marriable

Reacquiring marriable.com signal . . .

marriable

▾ Taking the Desperate Out of Dating

Hayley and Michael DiMarco

Grand Rapids, Michigan

Signal reacquired. Please proceed with this special wireless edition of marriable.

Published by Fleming H. Revell
a division of Baker Publishing Group
P.O. Box 6287, Grand Rapids, MI 49516-6287

Second printing, December 2005

Printed in the United States of America

Library of Congress
Cataloging-in-Publication Data
DiMarco, Hayley.
Marriable : taking the desperate out of dating / Hayley and Michael DiMarco
p. cm.
ISBN 10: 0-8007-3083-6 (pbk.)
ISBN 978-0-8007-3083-3 (pbk.)
1. Man-woman relationships—Religious aspects—Christianity. 2. Dating (Social customs)—Religious aspects—Christianity. 3. Marriage—Religious aspects—Christianity. I. DiMarco, Michael. II. Title.
BT705.8.D56 2005
646.7'7—dc22
2005012061

Published in association with Yates & Yates, LLP, Literary Agents, Orange, California.

Your in-store savings:
Huge! Just huge!!

Your local branch designer:
Mr. Brian Brunsting

Thank you for shopping at www.hungryplanet.net

up early
pay credit card
buy milk (on sale for $1.99)
get flowers - pink

Wash car
pickup some lunch or have leftovers

Buy some books for vacation
- Dateable
- Mean Girls
- something from the "Dirt" series?

Shave!
Use deodorant!
- bring flowers
leave at 5:45 to be there at 6:00

Lots of Results **marriable**

Sort by:

Chapter

Title

Author

Keyword

Organize by:

Putting stuff in order

Random info blurbs

Alphabetical by title

Organize?

Distribute in certain categories:

Wicked keen

Really keen

Keenish

Plain keen

Stop saying keen

When:

Today

Tomorrow

Later

I said later!

When attempting this type of surfing,
we encourage you to leave your laptop
on the beach.

Surfing for Guys, Surfing for Girls

Surfing for Guys

BY HAYLEY

When I signed on to my first dating website, all I wanted was to meet people. I was so tired of working at home alone day after day and spending night after night curled up with a bowl of popcorn and *Everybody Loves Raymond*. Okay, maybe I just wanted somebody to love Hayley. So one day when I was too sick to work, I decided I wasn't too sick to surf, and I did it. I posted a profile on an Internet dating site. I never thought I'd do it. I mean, what was I, desperate? Me, an author of a book on dating for teens, resorting to posting my picture in hopes of getting a bite? But sickness can make you do crazy things, so I spent the requisite twenty minutes filling out the profile and posted my picture.

After I got through the heavy lifting, I was ready to surf for guys. I typed in my desired age range and hit search. Faces started to pop up, and I remember screaming something like, "Glory hallelujah, human men!" Granted, they weren't in the room with me, but they were somewhere looking for someone, and heck, that someone might just be me. On the first page I smiled. They seemed nice but not too hunklike. So I clicked

Username: haze
Last Logged On: July 2003
Location: Nashville, TN
Age: Thirty-something
Height: 5'11"
Status: Single
Occupation: Writer
Favorite Food: Spaghetti
Favorite Movie: *Wizard of Oz*
Pets: Two cats—Puppy & Pickle
Fav First Date: Anything with food!

"Next" and perused the sea of men. A California cutie popped up, and I clicked on his photo. His bio was interesting. Not perfect, but then, who is?

Over the next few days of my free trial, I started to get emails. They poured in, really. It was quite funny. I had found dating heaven, as easy as turning on my computer. I was hooked. I started responding to emails, checking out hopefuls. I even responded to some IM's. But on the fifth day of my journey, *he* showed up. His screen name was *bobismydog*. Cute. Not silly like *HunkforJesus* or *Yourguardianangel*. He seemed odd, kind of like me. So I bit. The generic pickup line, or "smile" as they call it on their website, he sent said, "Your profile gave me a smile, so I thought I'd send you one in return." Being new to Internet dating, I had no idea what he was talking about. Did my profile secretly email him and make him smile? Was I an aggressive Internet dater and I didn't even know it? So this was my response: "My profile smiled at you? Behind my back? Bad profile!" *Send.*

His photo was hunky but in a very funny way. It was him sitting next to some Disney monkey, making a monkey face. What, no shirtless stud standing next to his Corvette? No picture of him with his arm around some anonymous female that I must assume is either his sister or his ex-girlfriend? No, just a goofy photo of a maybe dreamy guy making a monkey face to the camera. My kinda man. Then his bio sent me over the top. He was just what I had prayed for: 6'2", dark-haired, Italian, from a big family, Christian, my age. At first blush, perfect. But then, that's what I was prone to think. With each cutie, the female psyche screams, "This is it! The man of my dreams has come!" We want so badly to be loved. We are so desperate for a mate that we can be overly optimistic, in my opinion. But this one was different. How did I know? Because he got my sense of humor. Cha-ching! He got it. He got me. In our first IM our timing was like Lewis and Martin. We were like scriptwriters for the cast of *Friends*. We clicked. We got each other. That's when I knew. That's when he knew. That's when we knew.

Surfing for Girls

BY MICHAEL

I had tried Internet dating and singles websites before and met some nice women, but most of my dating habits were all wrong. I dated for the wrong reasons, and meeting people online didn't change any of that behavior, just the medium. So after taking a break and focusing on my job and its travel-intensive schedule, when I wanted to get back in the game, the only realistic option I had was to jump back online. But this time I was determined to pinpoint compatibilities beyond hair color and child-bearing age. I signed up for a free seven-day trial, posted a tongue-in-cheek profile with a goofy picture, and then left on a business trip. Much to my surprise, when I logged back on four days later, my inbox was full of inquiries and love notes from women I had never met. Part of me said, "Right on!" and another part of me said, "Whoa, look at all the desperate chicks."

Username: bobismydog
Last Logged On: July 2003
location: North of Seattle, WA
Age: 37
Height: 6'2"
Status: Single
Occupation: Consultant
Favorite Food: Pizza
Favorite Movie: *Field of Dreams*
Pets: One dog—Bob
Fav First Date: Coffee & baked goods

One of the great things about this particular dating site was that you could browse the members' profiles *and* it would calculate a percentage match based on how you rated the most important aspects of what you wanted in a date. The service would then send me snapshots of new members who met my criteria above a certain percentage match. Now, I had received a bunch of matches in the 60 percent range, but on the eighth day of my seven-day free trial, I was emailed an 80 percent match. *Eighty percent? No way,* I thought. I clicked on "Haze's" profile and saw she was of the same faith I had reintroduced into my dating criteria, lived in a city I traveled to often, and was a writer. She even used wit in her profile. Bonus, she was drop-dead beautiful.

Since my free trial was over, the only contact with Miss 80 Percent I could make without paying was to send a cheesy predetermined pickup line that the web service created for just such a situation. I chose the blandest of the bunch: "Your profile gave me a smile, so I thought I'd send one in return." That was way safer than "Is there an airport nearby? Because my heart just took off." Since Hayley's account was still free, she sent an email to my account. An email that I *couldn't read* because I had to pony up and pay to find out if she was the woman of my dreams. Ugh! I have to pay to potentially be rejected? So I tagged my credit card for $20 and got her email, which said absolutely nothing. Nice. But I must say I found it much more intriguing than the email I got just the day before that stated, "I know we've never met and we live 2,000 miles apart, but I think you're the man I'm supposed to marry." Since I'm a guy and love the thrill of the chase, I knew that "Haze" was a fox worth chasing.

As it turned out, we had a ton in common, great chemistry, and depth on important issues of life from our first chat online. The only question that needed unraveling was were we going to make the same mistakes of our dating pasts, or would we write a new chapter with the lessons we'd learned? Come to find out, we would learn together how to write the book on being *Marriable*.

Swans mate for life.

We wonder if they argue over joint checking.

Why *Marriable?*

Marriage: What's the Big Deal?

You don't have to look further than Donald Trump, Elizabeth Taylor, Britney, and J.Lo to realize people feel some undeniable pull toward getting hitched. The question is, why would so many celebrities with so much to lose financially and emotionally repeatedly go back to the altar to try marriage again and again? It can't be the undercurrent of morality that runs through Hollywood's elite. Society certainly has very little moral or emotional stigma left toward being unmarried and sexually active, not to mention living with your "significant other" (now there's a romantic term). Either marriage has become passé or we're missing something of the purpose and "inexplicable" pull to matrimony in spite of the 50-50 chance the wedding day will soon lead to divorce court.

If you picked up this book wondering just who it's written for, well, it's for anyone who is not married but wants to be married someday. Whether you're juggling ten love interests or haven't had a date in three years, this book is for you if you want to understand yourself, understand the opposite sex and how you relate to them, and identify areas where you may be acting desperate in your dating life. And did we mention get more dates?

Juggling often requires standing on one foot and painting your face white.

Figure 1.1

People are constantly coming up with new formulas for dating and meeting your mate that will hopefully divorce-proof marriages later on—like be friends first, measure forty-six levels of compatibility, include your family in the decision making, and the list goes on and on. The message you will hear us say throughout this book is that **no magic formula can help you find the perfect mate, let alone divorce-proof your future marriage**. While we will share tips, tricks, and little-talked-about traits of men and women that will help you in your search, we're here to help reshape your whole outlook on dating and marrying the opposite sex. Because if you don't change what you're doing, you'll keep getting what you've got.

You've Got Quotes X

No magic formula can help you find the perfect mate, let alone divorce-proof your future marriage.

The last chapter of *Marriable* will cover our views on marriage, divorce, and true compatibility. The rest of *Marriable* covers what to do from now until you get engaged—i.e., what to do to take the desperate out of your search for "the one." If you want premarital counseling advice or to do research on marriage, this ain't your book. A number of other great books out there cover what to do from your wedding day on; log on to www.marriable.com for a list of resources on marriage. In short, this book will help you find someone who has a common approach to dating and definition of what marriage is and isn't. And if you and your future mate have the same definition, approach, and perspective, that's the one big herkin' compatibility that transcends religion, social standing, background, and where you like to vacation.

But until that last chapter, let's have some fun taking the desperate out of dating and pose the questions: Are you *Marriable*? Are they?

www.marriable.com

LEGAL NOTICE

Any reference, or indirect allusion, to previous Hungry Planet books (like Dateable: Are You? Are They?) is on purpose. Oddly enough, it even seems to be encouraged by our marketing department. Granted, we've never actually seen our marketing department, or really know what they do, but if they're happy, we're happy.

And yes, our lawyer writes our contracts on yellow stickies.

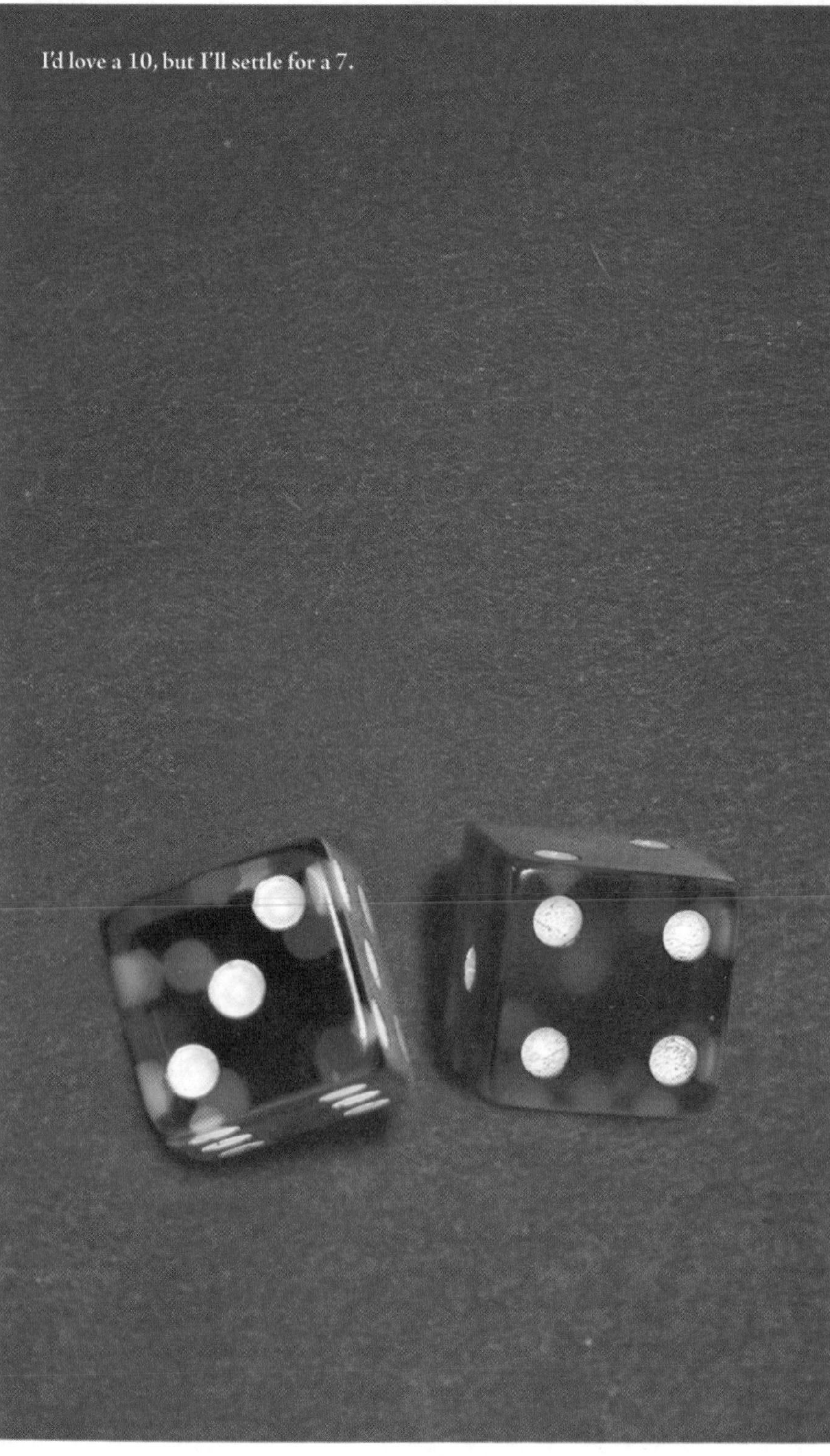
I'd love a 10, but I'll settle for a 7.

Playing the Game

> **That is why, no matter how desperate the predicament is, I am always very much in earnest about clutching my cane, straightening my derby hat, and fixing my tie, even though I have just landed on my head.**
>
> **Charlie Chaplin**

Okay, before we get started, let's settle something.

People always whine and complain about the games people play while dating. And though we agree that the use of mind games for evil is unacceptable, the real truth is that one effective way of approaching the dating ritual is to see that *it is a game*. And for the purpose of this book, we are going to do just that. Because not unlike a game, **dating should be fun and challenging**, with rules that make play fairer and more enjoyable for all. There are always winners and losers. And there are some unspoken rules, those things that make men and women respond in certain ways, that shouldn't be avoided or denied. These rules are what we'll call "laws of nature." They are behaviors, longings, and needs that traditionally have been associated with specific genders. We'll assume that your goal in the dating game is to determine whether or not you are going to marry your "opponent." After all, that's what dating was originally intended for. Therefore, we will all hereby solemnly agree that the object of dating is marriage. Any other kind of dating—for fun, giggles, or gropes—is unequivocally off the table for the rest of this book.

If dating is to be considered a game for the purposes of this discussion, then what we want to do is to consider the subtle nuances of playing said game that will allow us to ultimately win, i.e., marry. As Kenny Rogers says, "You gotta know when to hold 'em, know when to fold 'em, know when to walk away, and know when to run."

Michael,

Kenny also says, "Try my delicious fried chicken."

Hayley,

I knew having you write this book on an empty stomach was a bad idea, and we're only into the second chapter!

One of the reasons we refer to the *game* of dating is because this allows us to be less emotional and more objective—some might even say moral—in our approach to relating to the opposite sex. That said, we are not removing the emotional; it's essential to the dating process. What we are doing is tempering the emotional with logic, faith, and trust. Anyone who lives based on emotion only would be pretty hard to live with. We must always temper emotion with truth and use the gray matter we've been given. If we cull down all that is dating into a nice, simple game with rules and goals, then we give emotions less of a chance to persuade us and allow truth to reign over our decisions. When this happens the most amazing thing takes place: the load is lifted, the burden lightened. And dating becomes less about me and more about you. Please consider that *game* never means that dating is to be taken lightly but instead that it has natural laws and goals that, if honored, will produce great rewards.

As alluded to earlier, the dating game has rules, and these rules are simply a listing of the laws of nature that traditionally govern each sex. We're not going to get into whether these laws were arrived at by creation or by environment. What we will discuss is the fact that these laws do apply in most cases. In some rare instances, we might run into a male who lives by some of the laws that the female gender lives by and vice versa, but since these are the exception and not the rule, we will not apply them to the whole. Once again, working in generalities is much more fun and keeps our editor happy, since addressing every viewpoint or exception would make *Marriable* thicker than the pizza section of the Chicago yellow pages.

Hayley,

Sheesh! Do we need to stop so that you can eat?

Michael,

Don't make me choose between writing and pizza.

Okay, now that the legal mumbo jumbo is out of the way, let's take a closer look at playing the game.

The Object of the Game: Marriage

If marriage is the goal of dating, then it must be the goal for both parties. This is what is known as a win-win situation. If one wants to get married

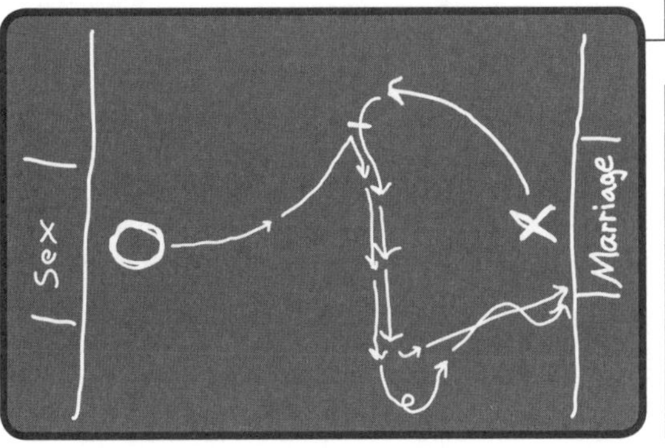

Typical M/F game plan.

Figure 2.1

and the other doesn't, you have a forfeit. Game over. No more play allowed. Fold up your board, collect your game pieces, and go home.

The Players: Male and Female

For the purposes of this book (and populating the planet), dating will be considered to occur between a male and a female.

Fairly typical pickle jars.

Male Roles
As the male, this player has the following strengths and weaknesses:
Opens pickle jars Doesn't ask for directions Least likely to cry Less expressive Less vulnerable The one who asks out The one who pays Looking for respect and appreciation Considers beauty in a mate important

Fairly typical cucumbers, which are really close to a pickle, just not quite so pickle-like.

Female Roles
As the female this player has the following strengths and weaknesses:
Eats pickles Loves to talk and connect verbally Enjoys being thought of as beautiful Gravitates to fuzzy creatures and that new-baby smell

Craves romance and gives points to the male for it

Is looking for companionship

Considers safety to be paramount

More expressive

More emotional

The one who is pursued

The Rules

Male and female. Each unique. Each different and yet potentially complementary. In an effort to understand how to play the game, we assume the following rules:

- Men were made to chase
- Women were made to be pursued
- Men are generally the main providers
- Women are the nurturers
- Men communicate differently than women
- Women want different things out of relationships than men

Take note of these. They will probably be on the test.

And finally . . .

- If you keep doing what you're doing, you'll keep getting what you've got.

Let's play!

We can howl for hours together.
He must be the one.

Desperate Lies Women Tell Themselves

> I am not yet desperate enough to do anything about the conditions that are making me desperate.
>
> Ashleigh Brilliant, American writer, cartoonist, columnist

> Women marry men hoping they will change. Men marry women hoping they will not. So each is inevitably disappointed.
>
> Albert Einstein, genius

We all lie at some point in the dating relationship. **It's just a matter of whom we lie to.** For some reason women have gotten really good at lying not to the man but to themselves. Women somehow find it easier just to ignore the truth—i.e., lie to themselves—than to face up to the fact that yet another man just isn't the one. That's why so many women stay in bad and even dangerous relationships when to the outside observer they so obviously need to get out. What these women do is concoct in their minds some big lie like, "Things are getting better," "It's really my fault he gets mad," or "I can't bear to be alone, so I have to put up with him." We've all seen it before, and it's nasty.

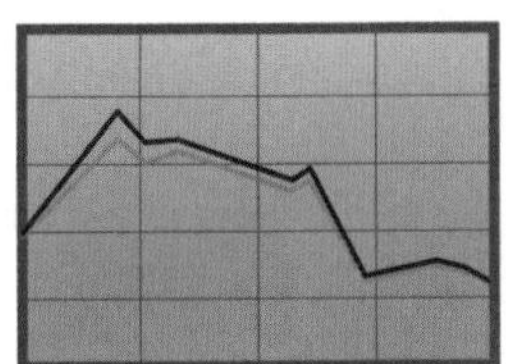

Average YTD performance of relationships in which women lie to themselves.

The woman who lies to herself looks as desperate as she is. But the lies women tell are not always that obvious to the woman herself. Sometimes the lies don't keep women in relationships; they keep them *out* of relationships.

Desperate Female Lie #1: "I'm waiting for Mr. Perfect."

The biggest of female lies is that Mr. Perfect is out there somewhere. Romance novels and chick flicks feed this lie like gas on a fire. The perfect man created by these genres of entertainment really doesn't exist anywhere but in the imagination of women. Men, just like women, are broken and fallen creatures; they have good days and bad days. They don't exist to make women happy, though they may have their romantic moments. But they will also have bad days when they make women mad, hurt them, or don't live up to their expectations. Men are human and should be respected as such. When a woman imagines (or lies to herself about) the perfect man, she suddenly squeezes out every man who isn't, well, perfect. And unless she's holding out for Mr. Jesus himself, the woman's going to be waiting a very long time.

Mr. Perfect. We have our doubts. We attempted to ascertain his true identity, but we just couldn't get that helmet off. He always insists on protection.

The healthiest way to overcome the Mr. Perfect syndrome is to consider what a mate is truly for. For decades women have bought the lie that men exist to fulfill their romantic fantasies. They exist to make women happy. But surely, when looking at it objectively, no woman can truly say she believes her man exists solely to make her happy. He is an individual just like she is, with wants, needs, and desires, and sometimes those things stand in direct opposition to the woman's. That doesn't make him wrong or evil; it just makes him human and, yes, sometimes a pain in the butt. He doesn't want to do what you want to do. He isn't as sensitive as you want him to be. He doesn't talk about his feelings. He doesn't want to shop with you every day. And the list goes on. This doesn't make him imperfect; it makes him a man! And when women demand, even of themselves, to find the man who fulfills them, they do both themselves and the man a disservice. Frankly, the only one big enough to fulfill you is God. He's the only one with the power and skills to do it. Putting that much weight on a man is a lie of epic proportions. If you can just let go of the lie and start to accept the imperfections, weaknesses, and stinkiness of men, the world of dating will open up to you.

Sub-lie:
"Mr. Okay is better than no one."

At the other end of the spectrum is the woman who will lie to herself all day long about why she *can* accept this weakness or that character flaw in a man because of ____________________ (you fill in the blank). Many women will lie to themselves about his nasty behavior just to keep the relationship going. Here are a few of those lies that women tell.

Desperate Female Lie #2: "It's all about me."

Face it, you've believed it: the success of this relationship is all about you. The last girlfriend just wasn't good enough for him. You love him more, you're better for him, you make him a better man. It doesn't matter what he did or why they broke up. The real reason he broke up with those other women is because *they* didn't know how to treat him. You know the reason he has never settled down, stayed married, or made the commitment in the first place is because they didn't know how to make him happy. But you do! *You* know what he needs.

Hayley,

Oh, how many times I've thought this in my dating past. I was sure *he wasn't dysfunctional, he just hadn't dated me.* I would fix him. He'd want to settle down with me because I am different. Ha! That didn't work out too well for me. It wasn't till I got more realistic that I finally landed the man of *my* dreams.

As a woman you want to be the best he's had. And you know that no matter how many "victims" he's left in his path, he'll somehow be nicer to you than he was to all the others because he really cares about you. Those girls were witches, and now they are just jealous. They weren't good enough. You know he chose *you* because you are better for him and more important to him.

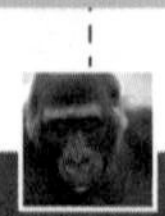

Michael,

Yeah, I've been on the other end of that equation—wishing I were man enough to break up with her and all the while thinking that she would have the common sense to break up with me. But the lies kept coming in her mind, evidently. No matter what I did, I just couldn't get her to see how bad I was for her. I was a twisted puppy, no doubt, but it really is mind-boggling how much you have to mess up to get a woman to break up with you.

Ladies, listen to the exes. If they all say he was a jerk, they are not saying it because they are jealous. They are saying it because he was a jerk. He is going to treat you the same way he treated the others. The issue is not *your* value but *his* character.

Remember, yellow and red flags are to alert you that you could face a problem and you need to be observant. They aren't always signals that those are parts of his character that you're there to change. Speaking of that . . .

Desperate Female Lie #3: "I'll change him."

Oh, what woman hasn't uttered these words? It's in the DNA makeup bag or something, this lie that all he needs is *you* to be a better man. "He has never changed because he has never had someone to change *for*. But he will want to change because of how much I love him. I will be able to make him better. He will become Prince Charming, and I will be his princess." Ah yes, the battle cry of the delusional.

Let's just say this now: you can't change him. It doesn't matter how much you want to or try to. He will not change for you. Oh, sure, he may show progress. He may even look like he *has* changed. But if he changed for *you*, as soon as you break up he will go back to doing the same things because he'll have no more need to please *you*.

And then you'll really lie to yourself and think, *Oh, he needs me,* because when you are not with him he goes back to doing stupid things. That's not it. The thing is, just like women lie to themselves, men will lie to get what they want. And this includes lying in what he does just to please you temporarily. The truth of the matter is that real change comes when *he* wants to change, not because *you* want him to. So don't convince yourself that you have to be with him to make him better. If that is the case, he hasn't changed. He is just putting on a good show.

From the man's perspective, don't think he doesn't know you want him to change. He's not as dull as you may think. When he senses you want him to change, his ego takes a nosedive. And he starts to feel like less and less of a man when he's with you. After all, if he were the man he was meant to be, you wouldn't have to work so hard to change him, he reasons. The feeling

Hayley,

Okay, I have to chime in on this one too. I actually did this. A guy once told me a bunch of women he had dated had banded together to form a "hate club." Now, I knew this wasn't literal, but the fact that he got a kick out of telling me that all his previous girlfriends now hated him should have been a red flag to me. But that was way before I was anywhere near being *Marriable*, and I paid the *unMarriable* price for it: heartache! And I should have seen it coming.

Hayley,

One of the things I liked about Michael was his ability to admit the mistakes he had made and his humility about them, unlike the guy who laughed about it. Michael told me of his past but showed me in his actions and character that he had grown and changed. So you don't want to give all guys a life sentence for their stupid years. (MICHAEL: Or decades!) But time and testing will prove if they are truly repentant and changed men.

is both ego-deflating and claustrophobic at the same time. The last thing a man wants is a woman who wants to change him. So if you see several things about him you want to work on changing, then work on dating another guy, because this one's probably not the one for you. Love means accepting the loved one for who they are, not who you imagine they can become.

Desperate Female Lie #4: "It's the other woman's fault."

When a man cheats on a woman, something amazing often happens. More times than not she gets madder at the female who "lured him away" than she does at her man. She's ready to rip that woman's head off. She can't wait to tell her friends all about the slut who went after her man. "After all," she reasons, "he wouldn't have done anything if *that woman* didn't make the first move." The lie is that it didn't take two to tango, it only took *her*, that seductress. But surely in a moment of sanity one can realize that the man is more to blame than the interloping woman. After all, he is the one who supposedly was in love with one woman while seeing another. *He* is the weak link in the relationship, not the sleazy, man-stealing female.

This happens all the time. The other woman gets blamed, chased down, talked to. And for some unknown reason, the girlfriend puts the man into a forced relationship "break." He gets the cold shoulder; she won't return his phone calls or have anything to do with him for a time. But once he

Hayley,

I remember one time in college I went on a date with this guy—one date. And a few days later his girlfriend, of whom I knew nothing, tracked me down and called me. She accused me of trying to steal her man, called me a few names, and told me never to see him again. As I look back I think, *How odd that she got mad at me, the girl who didn't know he had a girlfriend, when all the while I'm pretty sure the guy she was fighting for knew he had a girlfriend.* It's a mixed-up world!

Michael,

Man, I didn't know you dated so many players!

Hayley,

Yeah, I just had to wait for one to retire before I'd marry him.

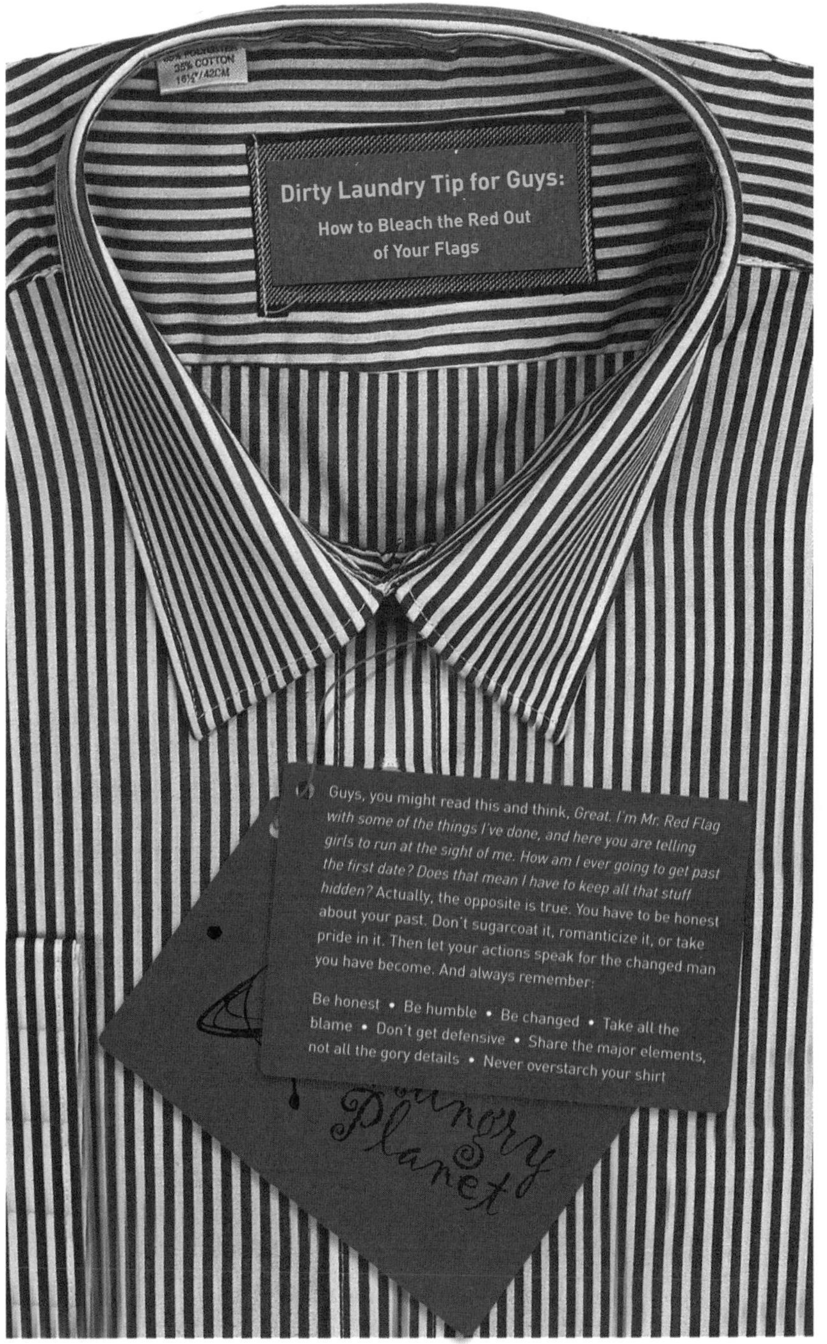

Dirty Laundry Tip for Guys:
How to Bleach the Red Out of Your Flags
Guys, you might read this and think, *Great. I'm Mr. Red Flag with some of the things I've done, and here you are telling girls to run at the sight of me. How am I ever going to get past the first date? Does that mean I have to keep all that stuff hidden?* Actually, the opposite is true. You have to be honest about your past. Don't sugarcoat it, romanticize it, or take pride in it. Then let your actions speak for the changed man you have become. And always remember:
Be honest • Be humble • Be changed • Take all the blame • Don't get defensive • Share the major elements, not all the gory details • Never overstarch your shirt

Affair
+ Dog house
+ "I'm sorry"
= Got away with it
repeat

has proven himself and she's convinced that he has "learned his lesson," she softens up on him. She reasons, "Now he realizes how important I am to him and that he can't live without me. So I'll give him a second chance." And another lie takes root in the female psyche. The "slut," of course, will never be forgiven for what she has done, but the man, well, she's sure he is sorry.

The truth of the matter is, she didn't teach the guy how valuable she is to him. She taught him that he can cheat and get away with it. She showed him that he can cheat, blame the other girl, be in the doghouse awhile, and in the end everything will be forgotten once she's convinced he has learned his lesson. It's a great scam for men, really. They just have to let the woman talk herself into believing her own lie. The man gets off the hook, and the other woman becomes public enemy number one. And the girlfriend has been played like a cheap guitar.

Desperate Female Lie #5: "He didn't mean to."

A desperate woman will excuse all kinds of behavior: "He didn't mean to hurt my feelings, but he had a bad day at work and was depressed." "He didn't mean to hit me. He was upset, and I shouldn't be nagging him when he is upset." "The reason he drinks so much is because he lost his job and that is the only way he can deal with it."

A desperate woman will excuse any behavior from a man as long as he has a reason. This is a major self-deception. *Every* action has a reason.

Good or bad. Big or small. And a man can come up with a good-sounding reason for everything he does. *The desperate woman just needs an excuse to believe in so she can justify his actions and keep the dream alive.* Being upset is never an excuse for lashing out at someone. A healthy woman knows this and won't allow a man to use *any* excuse to be hurtful or violent. And repeatedly telling him "I just won't stand for this!" but then accepting his "I'm so sorry" is just as much of a lie as not saying anything to him in the first place. A healthy man might need correction occasionally, but it won't happen time and again. If bad behavior has become the norm, then consider the lies you are telling yourself about his behavior.

Desperate Female Lie #6: "Sex will make him love me."

It's a tale as old as time: women give sex to get love, and men give love to get sex. But women have to understand that sex doesn't equal love to men. A man doesn't want to have sex with you because he loves you so much. He wants to have sex with you because he wants to have sex. Sure, it will mean a lot to him. Just like the last one meant a lot to him and the next one will mean a lot to him—in other words, sex means a lot to him.

A man doesn't want to have sex with you because he loves you so much. He wants to have sex with you because he wants to have sex.

Marriage as an institution exists in part to protect the sexual relationship of a couple. It's a commitment whereby a couple agrees that they will protect one another's honor both in and out of bed. Many might scream, "But marriage doesn't protect anything when over 50 percent of them end in divorce." To that we say, "But how many sexual relationships outside of marriage end?" Reason would suggest a great deal more than 50 percent. Chances are that if a man is willing to take sex from you before making a marriage commitment, he's done it before and he'll do it again. With a man, sex is your best bargaining tool, so don't waste it on anything less than a ring, a dress, and a cake. Sex is the number one motivator for men in making a commitment and taking a mature approach to relationships. Don't give up your biggest bargaining chip without a signed contract.

Michael,

Do you give good phone? Guys, this is really important for you to get. If you aren't really into a woman but you enjoy talking to her on the phone, you're setting yourself up for an awkward "define the relationship" moment when you didn't even think there was a relationship.

Desperate Female Lie #7: "We can talk for hours! He must be the one."

Not all lies are obvious. Some are subtle. They are a bit harder to spot, but they are still lies. Like the conversation lie. A woman gets on the phone and has a great conversation with a man, and a funny thing happens: the longer he stays on the phone, the more she feels like he really digs her.

Hayley,

Yeah, this was a hard one for me to wrap my mind around because conversation really equals intimacy to us girls. We find it impossible that with such great convo he wouldn't be totally into us.

INSTANT MESSAGE
from bobismydog@marriable.com

See *How Being Just Friends Is a Waste of Time*, **page 75**. ☹

After a really long conversation, the woman calls her girlfriend to tell her how amazing he is, all because they talked so long. She proceeds to give her friend the play-by-play of the entire phone call.

The guy gets off the phone from one of those conversations and thinks, *Oh, I have to get back to real life and see if there's a game on.* He collapses on the couch next to his buddy without saying a word to him and watches the game. She's energized from being the prey, and he's exhausted from the chase.

Young men, you've mastered the phone-saber, now beware of the dark side of talking for hours.

Desperate Female Lie #8: "It's okay if I call him."

Women also buy the subtle "It's okay if I call him" lie. She's got her eye on a man, but he isn't making a move. Women will convince themselves that "maybe he's just shy. He likes me, but I'm going to have to make the first move. It's okay. What do I have to lose?" Well, you mean besides his respect?

The underlying lie she tells herself is "There is no way for me to get a guy other than going and getting one myself. If I never call, no good guy will ever call me." That's just not true. Sure, lazy men might never call, but who wants a lazy man?

Here's the way it is: men lose interest quicker when women call. And it's in direct proportion to how much they call. Deep down, men know women want commitment—maybe not today, maybe not tomorrow, but the fact remains that

Hayley,

Most of my life guys didn't have the nerve to call me. They were intimidated by me.

Michael,

So you wanted to date a guy without any nerve? You wanted a guy who wasn't man enough to date you? If he's too intimidated to call, he's too weak to date you. But honestly, maybe you were the problem. Maybe you needed to soften the things that intimidated them.

Hayley,

Touché. I was the tough broad. I had to lead. I was once told, "You'll need to find a man who can handle you, Hayley"—i.e., I was a handful. But aren't you glad I tamed myself a bit?

Michael,

The brutal truth is, if he doesn't ask you, it's because he doesn't like you or he's not man enough to ask. Either way, why would you settle?

more women want commitment than men, and probably sooner rather than later. So every time a woman calls, she gives a ringing reminder that she's desperate for commitment.

And the plain and simple truth is, in the early stages of dating, men feel intimidated by a woman when she acts like a man, doing all the pursuing. But if he's not calling, it's less about intimidation and more about straight men not wanting to date men no matter how pretty they are.

At first a guy might like a woman calling all the time. He'll be flattered. But the thrill of the chase ends prematurely and leaves a bad taste in his mouth when he's the one being pursued. It's like winning the game in the first move—it's boring. Guys like the challenge. They like the game, so don't let them win on the first play. It's like you're playing hide-and-seek and you're afraid the guy isn't going to find you, so you hide in the middle of the room. Ooh, what a rousing game that would be. Focus on the fact you want to play hide-and-seek, not on just being found. Give the guy time to enjoy the game.

Desperate Female Lie #9: "He's got another woman, so he must be hot."

Another popular lie is seen in action among the ladies when a not-so-hot guy shows up with a nice-looking woman and the female radar in the room suddenly finds him more attractive. For decades men have known that if you want to catch a woman, you have to *have* a woman. As sick as that sounds, it's true. A man with a woman seems to have some sort of recommendation. He has credentials. Some women mistakenly believe that if another woman is with him, he must have something unseen, something about him that is important to women. It's a weird psychological phenomenon, but something inside of women ignites when some dork they've seen day in and day out suddenly walks in with a beautiful woman on his arm. They wonder, *Did I miss something?* But the truth is, this is just another lie women tell themselves to get what they want: Mr. Perfect.

Michael,

Guys, this one has a secret message in it for you: it often takes having a woman to get a woman. So don't take yourself out of the dating pool just because you aren't finding your dream girl. An active social life increases your chances of finding her.

Hayley,

True. And it's not being a player as long as you aren't stringing along one of your "friends" who might really wanna be more than friends. This is about going on one or two dates to see if something is there and then moving on. It's about you using the dating process to become more *Marriable* and gauging your *Marriable* net worth. It keeps you active and helps you become more and more of the man women will want.

Desperate Female Lie #10: "I just need to find a 'nice guy'!"

After women have had nothing but bad luck with men, they oftentimes blame it on the bad boy syndrome—dating only men who are bad for them—and mistakenly think that if only they could find that one nice guy, then things would be different. While it is true that if you continue to date broken men you will continue to have broken relationships, solving your dating problems is not as easy as just looking for a "nice guy."

The trouble is that the nice guy will disappoint you just as much as the bad boy did, because the nice guy will seem like a pansy, a smothering fool who won't leave you alone and loves you too much. The woman who has grown accustomed to being with dangerous men longs for the wild side, and the nice guy won't offer her that. What she really needs is a "good guy," a man who is still all male but also able to be kind and caring.

He is the man who doesn't use his masculinity to pound down the woman but doesn't hide it either. He isn't some kind of lap dog at her beck and call, and he isn't the bad boy who lives only for himself. This guy is a much better fit for this woman and will complement her better than the other alternatives. But if the woman simply thinks she has to find the nice guy, she will end up just as disappointed as she was with the bad boy.

INSTANT MESSAGE
from haze@marriable.com

See *Nice Guys Really Do Finish Last*, **page 145.**

Turning from Desperate to *Marriable*

When women lie to themselves, they become desperate—desperate to try to make the outside world fit the fantasy they have created. And in the end they not only look desperate, they *are* desperate. If you want to take the desperate out of your dating game, remove the lies you have been letting yourself believe. Face reality head on and don't be deceived by the way you'd *like* things to be.

Stock photo.
This is not everyday life.

All of these female lies boil down to one thing: romance. Every lie comes with the hope for romance and the dream that he will think about you constantly and be so into you that he can't get you off his mind. It's the delusional world of the romantic.

Once a woman starts being honest with herself, she becomes more beautiful and less desperate. Men

Thou Liest Down in the Green Pastures of Thy Mind

by Michael

All you women crave romance, and that is not a bad thing. But when you start lying to yourselves and acting based on those lies, you destroy who you are. You rip apart your identity and your purpose. In believing these lies, you essentially devalue yourselves and become less the kind of woman a man wants to fight for. You just need to be truthful with yourselves. Step back Jacqeline and see what lies you are believing.

Women are always telling me they want control (Janet Jackson comes to mind), but they won't take control of their thoughts, actions, or wardrobe malfunctions. Look for the truth. Don't just follow your emotions. Take what men say at face value instead of trying to figure out what we "really mean."

Women, don't continue to lie to yourselves. When you stop the insanity, it's shocking how *Marriable* you can become.

are attracted to a woman who is confident, smart, real, and honest with herself. She has a glow about her, an aura that attracts people. She becomes more elusive and therefore more sought after. The truth is that people want what is rare and hard to get. That's why engagement rings tend to be made out of diamonds instead of gravel from your driveway. A woman is a unique beauty, and once she has confidence she becomes incredibly more *Marriable*.

You can't get other people to stop lying to you. But you can stop lying to yourself. So many of the lies we've talked about here are torturing your soul and making you look desperate. The grand deception women weave for themselves is usually at the root of all their heartache. Relationships between men and women would go so much better

Looking at the World through Romance-Colored Glasses

by Hayley

A funny thing happens when you talk to couples separately and ask them about their relationships. Oftentimes what you hear from one is very different from what you hear from the other. I recall the romantic dream one woman wove while telling me of her wonderful relationship. She made it sound like the man would kill for her. His words were elegant and devoted, his actions grand and loving. But when I later talked to the man, I felt as though I were hearing about a completely different relationship. He said things were okay. He showed no signs of undying devotion. His portrayals of their encounters were everyday, mundane descriptions that left me wondering how they could translate the same relationship so differently.

As I watched the relationship crash and burn over time, I remember thinking that perhaps the man's unromantic view of their time together was the more realistic portrayal and the woman had deluded herself into imagining that what she had was just what she had always wanted. Either way, I can surely tell you that in most relationships, the man is not seeing things in as romantic a light as the woman is, and this does something to color the outcome of each relationship. Women would be on much more equal footing if they would refuse to weave a romantic web of intrigue where it doesn't exist. Romance is wonderful, but to overindulge our senses in its pursuit oftentimes means seeing it where perhaps it just isn't.

Fishing, Manure, and Romance

by Michael

Guys view romance in a totally different light than women. In the secret world of guys . . . see, that's the whole point—we have no secret world! We basically see getting into a romantic stupor as the equivalent to getting drunk. It's a temporary, forced state where you can't function effectively in your day-to-day routine, let alone operate heavy machinery. Women see romance as a destination and a better way of life. Men see romance as an occasional diversion that we can sleep off the next day.

Romance to men is another tool in our shed. A tool to woo, a tool to win. Once the initial courtship is over and the woman is won, most men see romance as a tool no longer needed. This is where women get confused and say, "Why did you change?" We reply, "Because I caught you." If a guy goes fishing, he doesn't keep spinning his reel after the fish is in the boat. I know, I know, a woman is a precious rose that needs to be watered, pruned, and cherished. And romance is the fertilizer that makes you bloom. I gotta admit, there's something there for us guys to take away (and not just the fertilizer jokes). But I also can't deny that we're not programmed that way; we have no green thumb when it comes to romance. Most of the time we still see romance as the suit we wear on special occasions. It's two dates on a calendar, February 14 and our anniversary (when is that again?). As usual, with any thorny issue between men and women, the truth probably lies in the muddy middle ground. The nitty-gritty is that men need to use the tool of romance more and women need to expect a lifestyle of romance less. But just like women need to avoid expecting a life of romance, a *Marriable* man realizes a woman will wilt without fertilizer . . . er, I mean, romance.

if women would understand that lies are lies even if they really want to believe them.

The truth is a powerful thing, and we contend that the majority of relationship problems would be resolved if women and men would look at things more realistically.

I never thought I'd find you (on sale).

Men Lie to Get What They Want

> I love you, and because I love you, I would sooner have you hate me for telling you the truth than adore me for telling you lies.
>
> Pietro Aretino,
> sixteenth-century Italian author

> Half the lies they tell about me aren't true.
>
> Yogi Berra

The Parable of the Woodcutter

One day while a woodcutter was cutting a branch off a tree above a river, his axe fell into the river. When he cried out, God appeared and asked, "Why are you crying?" The woodcutter replied that his axe had fallen into the water and he needed the axe to make his living.

God went down into the water and reappeared with a golden axe. "Is this your axe?" God asked. The woodcutter replied, "No." God again went down and came up with a silver axe. "Is this your axe?" God asked. Again the woodcutter replied, "No." God went down again and came up with an iron axe. "Is this your axe?" God asked. The woodcutter replied, "Yes." God was pleased with the man's honesty and gave him all three axes to keep, and the woodcutter went home happy.

Pickup Lines of the Desperate Male

- If I could rearrange the alphabet, I'd put U and I together.
- Are your legs tired? Because you've been running through my mind all day.
- Is your father a thief? Because he stole the stars from the skies and put them in your eyes.
- Are you from Tennessee? Because you're the only ten I see.
- Would you like to have breakfast tomorrow? Should I nudge you or call you?
- After checking the woman's shirt tag: Just as I thought—made in heaven!

This is NOT Jennifer Lopez. It's an axe that is height challenged (may also be referred to as a hatchet later in the book).

Some time later the woodcutter was walking with his wife along the riverbank, and his wife fell into the river. When he cried out, God again appeared and asked him, "Why are you crying?" "Oh, God, my wife has fallen into the river!"

God went down into the water and came up with Jennifer Lopez. "Is this your wife?" God asked. "Yes," cried the woodcutter. God was furious. "You lied! That is an untruth!"

The woodcutter replied, "Oh, forgive me, my God. It is a misunderstanding. You see, if I had said 'no' to Jennifer Lopez, you would have come up with Catherine Zeta-Jones. Then if I also said 'no' to her, you would have come up with my wife.

Had I then said 'yes,' you would have given all three to me. God, I am a poor man and am not able to take care of all three wives, so *that* is why I said yes to Jennifer Lopez."

The moral of this story is: Whenever a man lies, it is for a good and honorable reason and for the benefit of others.

Okay, the moral of the story is a lie as well, at least partially. Men lie to get what they want, and they only want two things:

1. To be admired
2. To be sexed

So while women are lying to themselves (see the previous chapter), men are lying to the women they're chasing. Whether the woodcutter lied because he was poor or because he dug J.Lo more than his wife, his lie fit into one of the two reasons above. Let us explain, Grasshopper. If he dug J.Lo's looks more than his wife's appearance, the woodcutter lied to get sex, ultimately. If he truly was concerned about not being able to afford three wives, he lied to avoid the shame of not being the provider for his (polygamous) family and the loss of admiration from his wives.

For now let's leave the sex issue for last and tackle why men lie to be admired.

Michael,

Frankly, I think between J.Lo and CZ-J, his buddies in the woodcutter's union might have had some admiration for ol' Bunyan.

Hayley,

But let's ignore those Neanderthals for now, 'cause it sounds like they'd probably lie to be sexed.

Michael,

True dat.

BBQ Spare Fibs

"Do you know where we're going?" asks the girl. "Absolutely. I think it's just over this hill," the guy says confidently. News flash: he's praying

Michael,

I remember when you met my buddies from my softball team. After the game we were hanging out replaying the game, exaggerating our individual feats . . .

Hayley,

Oh yeah! What did I say again?

Michael,

Honestly, I don't remember. I just remember the guys going "Ooooh!" tauntingly after you said it, and I went into Alpha Male mode, giving you a "whatever, you're a girl" attitude after that. A total jerk reflex.

Hayley,

I knew what I'd done right after I said it. I knew you were just saving face, and I didn't worry about it since you're just a guy. I just started making a list in my head of ways you would make it up to me. Only two more years and you'll be done with it too.

the exit he's looking for is over the next hill so he doesn't look like he's lost. Whether it's not stopping for directions, exaggerating about the size of the fish he caught, or opening the hood of the car on the side of the road pretending he knows what to look for before calling the tow truck, guys are deathly afraid of not being admired. This is especially true for a guy in front of his girlfriend and doubly true in front of his girlfriend *and* his buddies.

It's a fact, guys expect to spin tall tales with each other during ball games, cookouts, fishing trips, and the like. Somewhere in the testosterone-laden makeup of men, they fear being seen as the weakest in the pack and will do anything to stay toward the top of the pack pecking order. That's why when Jenni comes up to James when he's with his buddies and says, "I wuv you, hunny bunny," she's likely to get a colder shoulder than normal. If he offers his usual "I wuv you too, care bear," not only will that phrase be repeated at every guy event his buddies have for the next three years, but he also risks being labeled (*gulp!*) a girl. Hence he blows her off, saves face, and repairs the damage in private.

Lying to be admired also applies to the dreaded question, "What are you thinking?" Ladies, when a guy hears this question, he literally has to think about everything he's thinking that he can't tell you and then come up with something he can. Why? Because he doesn't want you to feel less important than his thought of how hilarious it would be if the moose head and other stuffed animals on the wall at the BBQ joint you're eating at started to sing *Bohemian Rhapsody*. He wants you to admire him, so he lies.

Ladies and liars, we're not justifying this rationale, we're just educating y'all on predictable male behavior. Girls, if you can show your admiration for your big strong man (even if he only benches 45 pounds), he'll dispense with a few of those little lies and still feel like leader of the pack.

Get Your Lies Down = Get Your Sex Up

Here's the seedier side of the lie guy. Once again, we wouldn't be surprised if this was part of the hormonal makeup of men, because seeding the planet is a pretty strong urge for guys. And lying to get sex is not a new concept. But before you say, "Oh, not my guy" or "Hey, I'm a stand-up guy with only honorable intentions," hear us out. If you've ever heard or uttered the following phrases, you've got a potential instance of a sex lie:

"I have never felt like this with anyone."
"I can't believe it's only been three dates."
"I never thought I'd find you."
"I'm going into the Peace Corps and I might not ever come back."
"Do you ever wonder if we're 'compatible'?"
"I love you."

While the woman is reveling in all of his whispered sweet nothings, the man is carefully observing his prey, knowing his words will make her feel good so that ultimately he will feel good. In the dietary nutrition of a relationship, the woman gets needed protein, but to the man his words are just empty calories. Ladies, if he's working this hard for something you've got, have you ever considered what happens inside his mind once he gets it? Touchdown! Remember, guys are all about the chase. Once the chase is over, a large part of the thrill is gone.

When a man and a woman have sex, the woman isn't doing herself any favors when it comes to finding out if he's the one. That's because sex is like an objectivity pause button for men. Guys put all questions like "Do I really see starting a family with her?" and "Can I live with her 'man hands'?" aside for repeated versions of the guy victory dance. Once the novelty of sex has worn off, he presses the play button again and resumes objectivity in assessing the relationship's chances. Then comes the breakup. All the while the woman is crying, saying things like, "But I thought we had this connection" and "What we had was so intense, so real." Women find out the hard way that the sex didn't increase his bonds of affection. When a woman has sex with a man (who isn't her husband) for the first time, she feels like the first chapter of life is beginning. For a man, it's like he just bought a brand-new book and read the last chapter first. Sure, he can read the first nineteen chapters after reading the twentieth, but he's going to get bored real quick because he already knows how it ends. Instinctively women know this. Women

This is a hatchet.

know intuitively that men like the chase and that their best bet is to stay one step ahead, just out of reach. But when a woman becomes desperate, she stops moving away from him and starts heading toward his bedroom. A woman needs to be a moving target, and men need to be practicing their aim, because once he's hit the target, he starts looking for the next moving target. When a woman has sex with a man, she feels a deep bond, a knitting of souls and purpose. When a man has sex with a woman, he becomes a one-track mind and puts getting to know the woman on hold in favor of getting to know her body . . . repeatedly.

Take it from me; if you let 'em get too close, it's all over. I always try to be a moving target.

Girls, does it creep you out a bit that this guy who's been buying you flowers, sending sweet IMs, and rubbing your feet is just in it for the big payoff? It shouldn't, because after all, he's just a man. Just remember that you can play him the way he was meant to be played by not rewarding the big fat horny liar until you get a ring, a cake, and a binding legal document!

Let's just accept this as fact for the "bad boys" and address the "nice guys" out there. *This still applies to you!* That's right. Even if you're one of those who is waiting for marriage (to which we say, there should be more of you), nice guys lie to be sexed too because, well, they're guys. No matter what a guy says, ladies, no matter how committed he is to taking things slowly, being respectful, being honorable, yada yada yada, *you* are the gatekeepers. No male on earth will ever evolve high enough to be trusted with the keys to the doughnut shop.

Hey "nice guys" out there. *This still applies to you!* That's right.

Mmmmm . . . doughnut.

Remember, when guys say, "I love you," they pretty much mean the same thing as when they say, "I love doughnuts" and "I love Brett Favre." The fact that he can have sex with you is just a bonus. The truth is, sex is the biggest bargaining chip a woman has in getting a man to commit; that's why it doesn't make sense to spend it before marriage. If you think about it, a compelling argument could be made that the sexual revolution ruined the chances for survival of committed marriages. And this isn't coming from a couple of prudes; we're speaking from two lives of mistakes, one broken marriage, and too many broken hearts. Yet we learned to handle our dating/sex life together pretty flawlessly. Don't get us wrong, waiting for sex was rough. But it was also definitely worth the wait.

Turning Desperate into *Marriable*

In most areas of their lives, guys yearn for control, and sex shouldn't be any different. Remember, a woman finds something incredibly alluring about a man who can exercise self-control despite all her feminine charms. She's not the only one who can be mysterious. That's hot. Old school is in, so show her how a gentleman rolls without losing your masculinity.

But ladies, just in case your guy doesn't take these words of advice, prepare yourself for lies desperately seeking admiration and sex. Hey, it's only natural. And gentlemen (if we can call you that), try a cold shower now and then, and consider investing in a GPS navigation system for your car. We bet you might just enjoy living a more honest life, and without a doubt you'll be infinitely more *Marriable*.

Hey, baby!
Yeah, right.

They Just Might Be Out of Your League

> I'm dating a woman now who, evidently, is unaware of it.
>
> Garry Shandling

Consumerism. The soul of a free market economy and essential to understanding our own *Marriability*. We all have money, we all spend it, and we all want to make sure we don't get taken in the process. In the fair exchange of goods and services, no one wants to be ripped off. It's just not kosher. We want to say, "Boy, I got a fair deal on this!" As far back as grade school we hear the mutterings of consumerism. For example, if I exchange my baloney sandwich for your banana only to find out that the banana is all brown and grody inside, you might hear me scream, "Hey, that's no fair! I gave you a perfectly good sandwich, and I got this nasty old banana!" All of us humanoids have a clear understanding of the word *fair*. And if we don't think the deal is fair, boy does the world hear about it. It's the law of the jungle—what's fair is fair—and we all know how to spot a fair deal.

The same rings true for the dating and mating scene. The queen of the prom isn't going to go shopping for the geek of the week and tell herself she's made a fair exchange in that deal.

No, we all know she's going to have her sights set on the quarterback. It's like two lunch boxes full of humans: "I'll give you a prom queen for that all-star!" And the deal is on. It's sad but true, and I hate to burst your bubble like this, but if you aren't a prom queen, you probably aren't going to get a quarterback. The kicker, maybe, but definitely not the quarterback. That's because we all have some kind of understanding of our inherent value. We all have this kind of unspoken tally of our *Marriable* worth. And if you've ever said, "She's out of my league" or "He won't give me the time of day" but you clamor after them anyway, you might just look totally desperate.

Let's look at it like this. On a scale of 1 to 10, where do you land? Be honest, now. Don't say you're a designer suit when you just fell off the bargain rack. Honesty is the first step in taking the desperate out of dating consumerism. What is your fair market value? If you said that you are an 8, then the best advice for looking for the love of your life is to look in the 8 range. Don't say, "I know I'm an 8, but I really love 10s, so I'll wander over to the 10 department and see if I can't blend in." You'll be spotted right away. And *bang*, suddenly you'll look like the desperate one because, well, uh, you are.

Due to the laws of nature, we all have some kind of understanding of where we fall on the *Marriable* scale, and we naturally expect to find someone who falls somewhat near to us. Then when we make the "ring exchange," we feel confident that we've gotten a good deal.

Hayley,

Hey, how did you rate me?

Michael,

Well, as far as "sexy, high-maintenance cat ladies" go, you were easily a 10! How did you rate me?

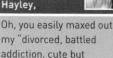

Hayley,

Oh, you easily maxed out my "divorced, battled addiction, cute but sarcastic" meter!

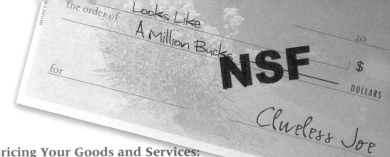

Overpricing Your Goods and Services: Writing Checks Your Body Can't Cash

We've heard stories of young men who for whatever reason think that they are clearly 10s. Sure, a guy may weigh a few extra pounds and not have terrific social skills, but at least he is an intellectual or spiritual giant. What woman wouldn't want him? And so he goes after every hot young thing that enters the break room or singles group, sure that she won't be able to resist his superior traits. But alas, he is powerless over her, and he retreats to the fridge and the determined opinion that "she just wasn't good enough." Oh, the cry of the relationally delusional. When you presume you have a higher *Marriable* quotient than you really do, you are bound for desperate failure.

In the dating process, giving yourself a fair market value is crucial. If you overvalue any of your qualities, you are sure to meet with repeated failure. And if you do somehow convince someone with a higher *Marriable* quotient than yourself to marry you, beware, because once they figure out your true *Marriable* quotient, they are likely to feel duped. Why do you think that over 50 percent of marriages, even ones based on moral values, end in divorce? Perhaps because one mate feels like they were lied to, swindled, or misled into believing that the other person was somehow more than they are. So in order to save yourself the grief, begin with a fair assessment of your net worth.

Assessing Your Market Value

To more clearly understand this *Marriable* consumer economy and your place in it, look over a few of the key features of a *Marriable* person and rate yourself. Circle your numbers:

Looks	1 2 3 4 5 6 7 8 9 10
Brains	1 2 3 4 5 6 7 8 9 10
Personality	1 2 3 4 5 6 7 8 9 10
Financial Stability	1 2 3 4 5 6 7 8 9 10
Spirituality	1 2 3 4 5 6 7 8 9 10
Charisma	1 2 3 4 5 6 7 8 9 10
Education	1 2 3 4 5 6 7 8 9 10
Hygiene	1 2 3 4 5 6 7 8 9 10
Ambition	1 2 3 4 5 6 7 8 9 10

Now add them up: ________

This is your *Marriable* quotient.

Your goal now is to find someone else with the same or close to the same quotient. Anyone with a much higher or lower number will be out of your range and leave one of you feeling duped. The essential thing to understand in the rule of consumerism is that the product (in this case you) has to be priced at a fair market value. Please note that this list of features isn't exhaustive. The list could go on and on, but what is important is that you consider the five to ten things that are of ultimate importance to you in a mate and then grade yourself on those. We all need and want a fair exchange. Here are some other things you might consider important.

Age • Smoker/nonsmoker • Denomination • Sense of Humor • Cleanliness • Anger issues • Upbringing • Political position • Kindness • Faith • Race • Social skills • Parenting ability • Cooking skills

Sexual Marketing and the Law of Consumerism

An often overlooked facet of *Marriable* consumerism is marketing. You might be overlooked by many "potentials" because they consider your *Marriable* quotient to be far below what it really is. What could be the reason for that? We're glad you asked. You might actually be portraying yourself in a lower range than you really are by the way you present yourself to the opposite sex. In this part of the dance, you must represent who you really are in a desirable way. Compare these two descriptions found in the classifieds:

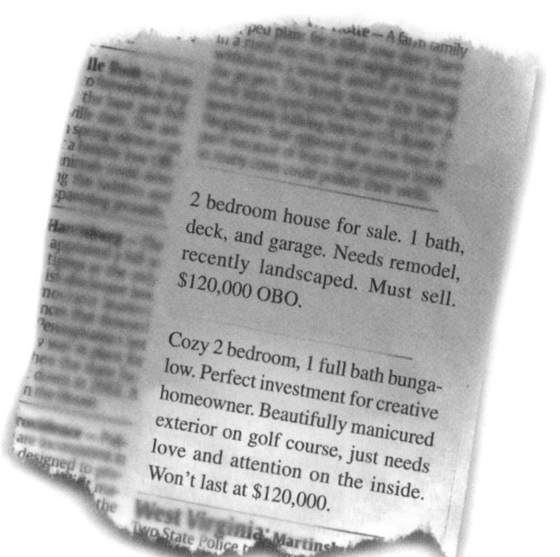

2 bedroom house for sale. 1 bath, deck, and garage. Needs remodel, recently landscaped. Must sell. $120,000 OBO.

Cozy 2 bedroom, 1 full bath bungalow. Perfect investment for creative homeowner. Beautifully manicured exterior on golf course, just needs love and attention on the inside. Won't last at $120,000.

System Resources

A few resources with different approaches on this issue of compatibility are *Rate Yourself on Romance* by Steven D. Kline and Amy Frome, *How to Know If Someone Is Worth Pursuing in Two Dates or Less* by Neil Clark Warren, and *The Birth Order Book* by Kevin Leman. For even more resources, go to www.marriable.com.

Both descriptions are of the same house, but which one makes the house sound more appealing?

As consumers we might think that products in TV, radio, and print ads are the only things marketed to us, but the truth is that we are marketed to and are marketing to others every day in the way we dress, talk, and reveal our inner selves. Like it or not, we are all in a continual dance of consumerism, presenting ourselves to the outside world so that they will see us for who we really are and appreciate our true value. The way we dress and groom ourselves tells the world who we think we are so that they can know us better and hopefully pick us as friends and mates. The concept of self-marketing is often overlooked and probably looked down upon by many, but don't put this book down and walk away just yet. Consider this: Let's say you're checking out a singles group at a local church. When you walk into the room, how do you decide who to talk to? What kinds of assumptions do you make about people based on how they look, how they smell, and what they wear? Certainly you make many. The girl in the corner wearing a tight top revealing two mounds of cleavage might tell you that she is fun, playful, sexual, looking for someone, and maybe not there totally for a Bible study.

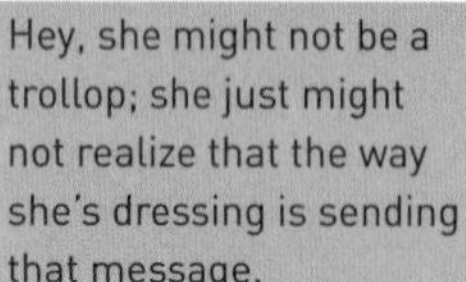

Michael,

Hey, she might not be a trollop; she just might not realize that the way she's dressing is sending that message.

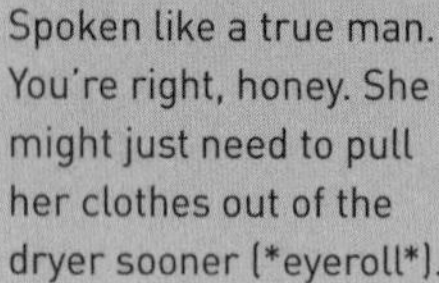

Hayley,

Spoken like a true man. You're right, honey. She might just need to pull her clothes out of the dryer sooner (*eyeroll*).

Now, this might not be intentional marketing, and that's the point exactly. We need to be more intentional and consider how we appear to others. Continuing our review of the room, the girl in the corner dressed from neck to ankles in an A-shaped dress, holding a Bible close to her chest, and looking down at the floor tells you another thing. Each person in the room decided what to wear that morning to show the world who they are and what they think about themselves. Subliminal marketing. It happens whether we know it or not.

So now the nagging question you have to answer is *How do you market yourself?* Does your target market, that group whose attention you want to get and are qualified to get, see what you have to offer? If you think you have a great mind, do you show it in your personality? If you consider yourself a fun person, do you show your fun side in the group, or do you wait in the corner for someone to come by and talk to you? Your *Marriable* quotient isn't something to keep hidden if you are ready to find the person of your dreams. It is something you need to allow others to pick up on so that the one who is just right for you will rise to the surface.

Michael,

I tell you, it's just like in that market in the Bahamas on our honeymoon—the barter system. The man who wants to close the deal says, "I'll give you a 10 in intelligence for your 10 in looks." To which the woman replies, "I'll take your 10 in intelligence and give you my 10 in looks if I can get an 8 in financial responsibility." "Wow," he responds, "I'll try to grow into an 8 in financial responsibility, but in the meantime I've got a 7 in earning potential, an 8 in spirituality, and a 7 in romance," and so on. In the end rings are exchanged and they "shake on it." Then the deal can't be broken when he says, "By the way, did I mention that I snore?"

Getting the Most Bang Out of Your *Marriable* Buck

If you know your *Marriable* quotient and you want to be sure that you get a fair deal and find someone who is quotient compatible, then you have a few more things to consider.

Looks Fetch a Pretty Penny

The fact that looks fetch a pretty penny is well documented. For evidence of this we have to look no further than the world of rock 'n' roll. For decades homely, skinny rock 'n' rollers have landed hot babes as wives and the world has asked why. *Marriable* consumerism is the answer. The rocker dude might score low in the category of looks, but his financial and charisma categories are, of course, off the charts. Added all together he might be less desirable than the girl he lands, but here's what happened. Rocker dude decided he would trade all of his points for a chick with looks. He didn't have any need for intelligence, kindness, spiritual fortitude, or compassion. So he put all his eggs into one sexy basket of looks. And that's what he got—a basket with no eggs, but a fine-looking basket it was. You have the same option. Well, not exactly the same, but you too can decide to put all your points into the looks category and fetch a fetching beauty in exchange for all your wonderful traits, allowing yourself to be gypped on the other categories like gentleness, intelligence, and character. **The thing to remember is that appearance is the most costly of qualities.** For some reason *Marriable* consumers put a lot of value in appearances, so they are willing to give up a few other qualities to have the looks they desire in a mate. The most ironic twist is that unlike other categories, looks are always guaranteed to fade!

The most ironic twist is that unlike other categories, looks are always guaranteed to fade!

A word to the wise: beware of putting all your eggs in one basket. The impact of beauty quickly wears off, and then where will you be when you want intelligent conversation or playful moments? Take a look around and you'll notice that people who are in love seem to find one another a lot cuter than others might say they are. In other words, the more you love someone, the hotter that person looks to you. Giving someone a chance to grow on you can add a lot of points to their looks category.

Sure, It's Got a Nice Paint Job, But How Is It Under the Hood?

Buyer beware! Before you commit to a permanent relationship with someone, you will need to consider your options. For this we will use the analogy of purchasing a car. Which features in a mate are the most important for you and which can you afford to skimp on? A realistic assessment of need will make your *Marriability* increase considerably. Regarding cars, we all know what we want and what we can afford. Marriage offers no lease terms, so since this will be a permanent purchase, we suggest that you consider all the features before you make the deal.

Performance

Don't kid yourself. Although you might desire the ultimate performance of a Ferrari, you might not be able to control it at the speeds it was designed for or afford all of the speeding tickets that you would get with it. When selecting a mate, you need to consider what kind of performance you are looking for. Do you want someone who can be up all night with you partying, dancing, staying out with friends? Maybe someone who enjoys rock climbing, mountain biking, and ice fishing is right up your alley. Or do you prefer a quieter partner who is content to stay home and watch TV or read a book every night? Think about what kind of performance you are comfortable with and look for the best fit for your needs. Evaluating your performance needs can help you focus on where to meet *Marriable* candidates to fit your lifestyle.

Reliability

More often than not, reliability should be a key factor in determining which vehicle is for you. Sure, performance can be an attractive feature, but the real rub is reliability. Can you trust the car to get you where you need to go? Does it have a good reputation for reliability? Don't take your eyes off of the intended use. Will this purchase do the job you need done? Consider the reliability of your mate before you race into a commitment. Do they have a history of cheating, forgetting dates, or not doing what they said they'd do?

Aggressive Styling

You like a car that has the styling of a 200 mph Italian sports car. So how does that fit with your lifestyle, friends, occupation, family, and hobbies? For some people a flashy car is great for a week or two but not real practical for the long term. If tattoos and nose rings aren't commonplace in your work, social, and family circles, is that something you can live with? Same for bare midriffs, miniskirts, and fishnet stockings. (And if he's dressing that way, girls . . . *run*!)

Fuel Economy and Scheduled Maintenance

With the rising cost of fuel, one has to be conscientious of fuel economy. How much will running the vehicle cost you? Is it a gas guzzler or an economy vehicle? And does it matter to you? A $40 fill-up might not even make you flinch. Know what you feel comfortable paying at the pump before you walk the lot, and your search will be narrowed down considerably. Does she only like to dine at the finest restaurants and wear the latest designer clothes? Are his injuries from his extreme sports lifestyle constantly keeping him in casts and on crutches? Can you handle all the emotional and financial costs involved with dating her? Is he constantly borrowing money from you? These costs must be figured into your *Marriable* budget.

That New Car Smell

Mmm! The smell of a new car cannot be duplicated. It's a delight to the senses and some-

Hungry Planet
New Husband Scent
NEW!
The patent pending
Hungry Planet air freshener
gives you that
new husband smell.
The previous scent,
"just friends potpourri,"
has been discontinued.

thing we all wish we could have in our car, but that isn't always an option. Sometimes the car you fall in love with isn't new. It's been driven and driven hard, and the new car smell has long since worn off. The car has some door dings, a rock chip in the windshield, and a mystery stain on the passenger side floorboard. As a consumer, you make the important decision of whether you can live without that new car smell for a lower price. Can you be happy in a used vehicle knowing that the newness was given to a previous owner? Can you deal with someone who has a long, not-so-distinguished sexual history? Are you okay with his kids visiting on weekends? Of course, sometimes a car with a salvage title is an amazing bargain, but most times you're looking at too many hidden repairs and headaches just waiting to happen.

INSTANT MESSAGE
from bobismydog@marriable.com

See *Restoration Projects*, **page 64**.

Mileage

When buying a used car, you should investigate that the mileage history is accurate—in other words, that there has been no odometer rollback. Many a seller has tried to fool a buyer by claiming that the car has less mileage on it than it actually has. Be sure you have all the facts. More mileage than reported can lead to unexpected problems in the future and an overall dissatisfied feeling about the purchase. If you haven't had time to find out about the mileage and the honesty of the seller, take time to get all the facts. Knowing if someone is telling the truth about who they were in the past and who they are now takes time and observation. If you didn't do the research before you fell head over heels, then it's time to start weaving the tough questions into your conversations, like "Tell me about your last relationship," "How do your relationships usually end?" and "That's a beautiful ring on your left ring finger. Who gave it to you?"

Seating and Cargo Space

Another feature of a vehicle is its space. How much room for growth do you see? Are you planning on growing a family? Will this car accommodate all your wants and needs? What kind of cargo space do you require? This will determine whether you buy a two-seater or an SUV. If you want to grow a family right away, you'll probably want to avoid someone with a jet-set career and go for the high school English teacher. A family can fit in a '70s station wagon as well as in a Cadillac Escalade. Do you require room for upward advancement in life, bigger cars, and bigger houses, or are you happy just where you are?

The Walk-Around

The final step before purchasing a vehicle is the walk-around. At this time you can look for any leaks or other telltale signs of needed repairs. Don't ignore the leak under the hood; in the end it might cost you more than you can afford. What we are talking about here is your engagement. Taking the time to have an objective mechanic—i.e., premarital counselor—ask you all the right questions can help you truly know if you and your vehicle are the right fit.

Restoration Projects

Some used cars have to be towed into the garage and might not be road ready for months or even years. Can you afford to garage your vehicle for that long and devote so much time and effort to restoration? Some restoration projects can still be daily drivers while being restored. They can be driven as normal and over time restored to their mint condition. This kind of vehicle can be enjoyed while being worked on. The thing to consider is that in a relationship, you aren't restoring the other person; the person is restoring him- or herself. Are they responsible and desirous of change? Do you trust them to improve themselves and do the work? Or will it all fall on your shoulders? That's a recipe for disaster. As always, *caveat emptor* (buyer beware). This is a decision you will need to make before you ultimately pick your dream vehicle.

Determine Where You Will Spend Your Marriable Buck

In conclusion, in the process of becoming more *Marriable,* you must determine where you will spend your *Marriable* buck and how much you have to spend. An accurate assessment of your investing power and an unwavering determina-

Hayley,

You know, this might sound crazy, but most people drive cars that represent what they're unintentionally selling. The guy driving a monster truck, the man driving the little convertible, and the guy driving the family sedan give three distinct impressions.

Michael,

It's true. Like that Honda commercial—people really do look like the cars they drive. If not externally, at least internally.

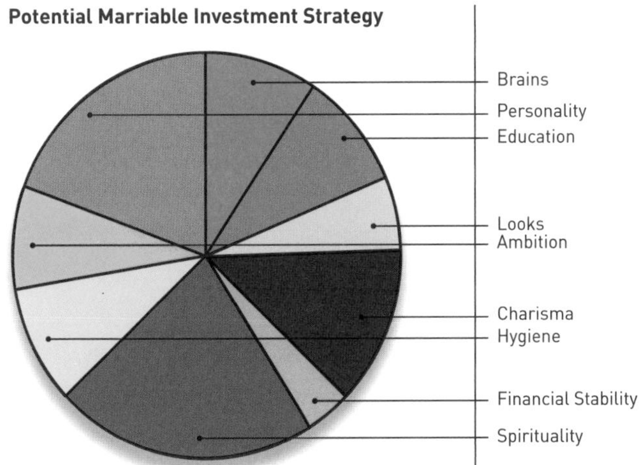

tion to spend on the essentials is sure to yield you a better result than all the lying to yourself in the world could ever fetch. As you begin to have a realistic view of your *Marriable* quotient, you will begin to see a world of *Marriable* partners open up to you.

Turning Desperate into *Marriable*

If you are continually saying that you are a good catch and you can't understand why you are still single, perhaps you need to look more realistically at your *Marriable* quotient. Sometimes well-meaning people score themselves off the charts and then don't understand why others don't give them the same score. Seeing that your numbers might not be as high as you had previously thought is a sobering but healthy fact that needs attention. If you are shopping for what you can't afford, you will forever be wondering why they don't see what a good catch you are.

But you must also consider *where* you are shopping. Perhaps the place where you are shopping doesn't offer people who hold your qualities in high esteem. In order for those around you to give you points for the things you hold essential, such as faith, intelligence, or humor, you need to surround yourself with people who weigh your qualities with the same significance as you. If the people you are around find faith unimportant, then giving yourself a 10 in that category won't do anything to make you more *Marriable* in their eyes, because faith isn't even on their radar. A realistic assessment of your strengths and weaknesses and the values of those around you will go a long way toward making you more *Marriable*.

How to Spot a Gigolo
by Michael

Back in the 1940s, right at the end of World War II, my mother was working as a dance instructor for one of the big studios in Hollywood, California. At their annual Christmas party, she was talking to her best friend when she noticed a long line of women all leading up to a male dance instructor standing under the mistletoe. Her friend, who was engaged, asked her if she was going to get in line. My mother replied, "You couldn't pay me to kiss that greasy Italian gigolo."

Within ten months, my mother, Joyce, married Massimo DiMarco. They enjoyed fifty-four years of marriage, five planned children, and one accident late in life—me.

Times have changed over sixty years, and the semi-honorable chivalrous gigolo has been replaced by the one-track-mind "player." Keep a watchful eye on your man when you see these telltale signs of a player:

- Seems to know every romantic place in town
- Every woman he meets calls him "charming"
- His phone rings (or vibrates) constantly and he rarely answers when you're around
- Long trips to the bathroom when you're on a date (returning phone calls)
- He tells you often he's just gotten a long-distance phone call he's "gotta take"
- He hates it when you "pop in" at his place
- His eyes dart to every skirt that passes by
- He says things that sound too good to be true
- He'll talk about your future during intimate moments but never in daylight
- Uses spiritual encounters to achieve intimacy

Sgt. DiMarco, 1st Gigolo Division, circa 1945.

No, he is NOT going to dial the number for you.

"I'm Dating Jesus" and Other Excuses Why You're Not Dating

"Jesus loves me, this I know."

"And that's why I'm dating him."

Unless this was uttered by Jim Caviezel's wife, it sounds pretty weird to the untrained ear. But this is a mantra being uttered by many a spiritual single waiting for God to drop their dream mate on their lap "in his time" and hoping to avoid hurtful dating consequences. Imagine if you applied this principle to your career:

> I believe God has one perfect well-paying job already chosen for me; therefore, I have no need to worry about searching for it. When the time is right, I know God will bring me together with that company's HR department, and I will miraculously have all the skills and experience needed. In the meantime I'm not hiding in a closet avoiding all places of business, but I'm living my life without the pressure of having to look for a job.

Sounds pretty ridiculous, right? Well, many singles are over-romanticizing their relationship with God to satisfy the same needs that got them into trouble on the dating scene. This craze that if you date you're not living biblically just doesn't wash either. Singles need to learn how to act around a hot stove, not tell themselves the kitchen is off-limits until God wants them to cook and expect that then miraculously they'll know how to cook the meal of their life. You want to live biblically? Have your parents arrange a marriage for you. Now *there's* biblical. Just make sure they get some good oxen in return. Whatever the manner of matchmaking (arranged marriages, courtship, or car dates), mating methods have always been considered social customs, not biblical commands.

Centuries ago it was oxen. Now the groom's parents pay for the rehearsal dinner.

But the religious aren't the only ones who rationalize putting off getting into the dating world. Other excuses are "I'm just focusing on my career," "There aren't any good ones left," and—we both fell out of our chairs when we heard an intelligent single woman in her fifties say it—"So many men from my generation died in Vietnam, I've decided that my soul mate died in the war before we could meet."

Now, sometimes these excuses are valid. Focusing on school, career, or caring for a sick loved one can consume all your free time. But most often these excuses are heard when people are tired of making mistakes or striking out in the dating ritual. But just because you get a speeding ticket and are involved in a fender bender doesn't mean driving a car is bad; you just need to go to driving school.

The one rationalization that most all of us can relate to is "the last one just hurt too much." If it's been a few weeks or months, that's understandable. But if we're getting into years, that's another story.

People do some pretty stupid things when breakups happen, things that we're embarrassed to look back on and scared to repeat, frankly. In her book *Why We Love*, anthropologist and author Helen Fisher has penetrating insight into why love unreturned gives us such blurred vision and inspiration to do such stupid things:

> The bewitched lover shows the three classic symptoms of addiction: tolerance, withdrawal, and relapse. At first the lover is content to see the beloved now and then. But as the addiction escalates, they need more and more of their "drug." With time they hear themselves whispering, "I crave you," "I can't get enough of you," even, "I can't live without you." When the lover is out of touch with the beloved, even for a few hours, he or she longs for renewed contact. Every phone call that is not from the beloved is a disappointment.
>
> And if the beloved breaks off the relationship, the lover shows all the common signs of drug withdrawal, including depression, crying spells, anxiety, insomnia, loss of appetite (or binge eating), irritability, and chronic loneliness. Like all addicts, the lover then goes to unhealthy, humiliating, even physically dangerous lengths to procure their narcotic.[1]

We contend that most rationalizations or spiritualizations for avoiding an active dating life are due to either *addiction* (not being able to control one's self) or *rejection*. If you find yourself making rationalizations for not dating, ask yourself, "What am I afraid of?" Fear of rejection can paralyze even people who seem to have everything going for them to the point that they won't even accept a dinner invitation from someone they are attracted to. Others may restrict themselves to "group dating" where they can find safety in numbers. They get to spend time with the opposite sex with everyone in silent agreement that no one will reject anyone else. It's kind of like a don't ask, don't tell lonely hearts club.

Having a healthy perspective and taking things slow in your dating life without letting things spiral down the road of love addiction can actually speed you into *Marriability*. Addiction is an absence of balance and perspective. Force balance into your dating life no matter how much you want to spend time with a new attraction. Cut the length of phone calls, and don't reserve every evening and weekend for your sweetie before you agree to meet up with your friends. As Mr. Miyagi said in *The Karate Kid*, "Balance is key, Daniel-San." Most people, when looking for a mate, notice early on if the other person has a healthy balance in his or her life. But you're not going to find a mate without the looking part.

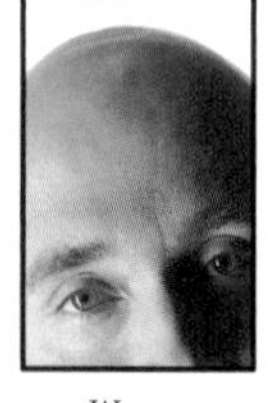

Wax on.

Wax off.

Turning Desperate into *Marriable*

Work, family, faith, exercise, fun, friends, and love.

When you have proper balance in your life and aren't afraid of dating anymore, you'll find that your newfound confidence in living life is a secret pheromone. Potential dates start coming out of the woodwork. But you have to be willing to risk looking for love and dealing with any issues of addiction and rejection. You shouldn't stop dating; you should stop fearing or obsessing. When you stop standing on the sidelines and get back in the game, you can begin to live a dating life that shows balance. Removing fear and tendencies toward addiction from your dating habits (not removing yourself from dating) makes you become truly *Marriable*.

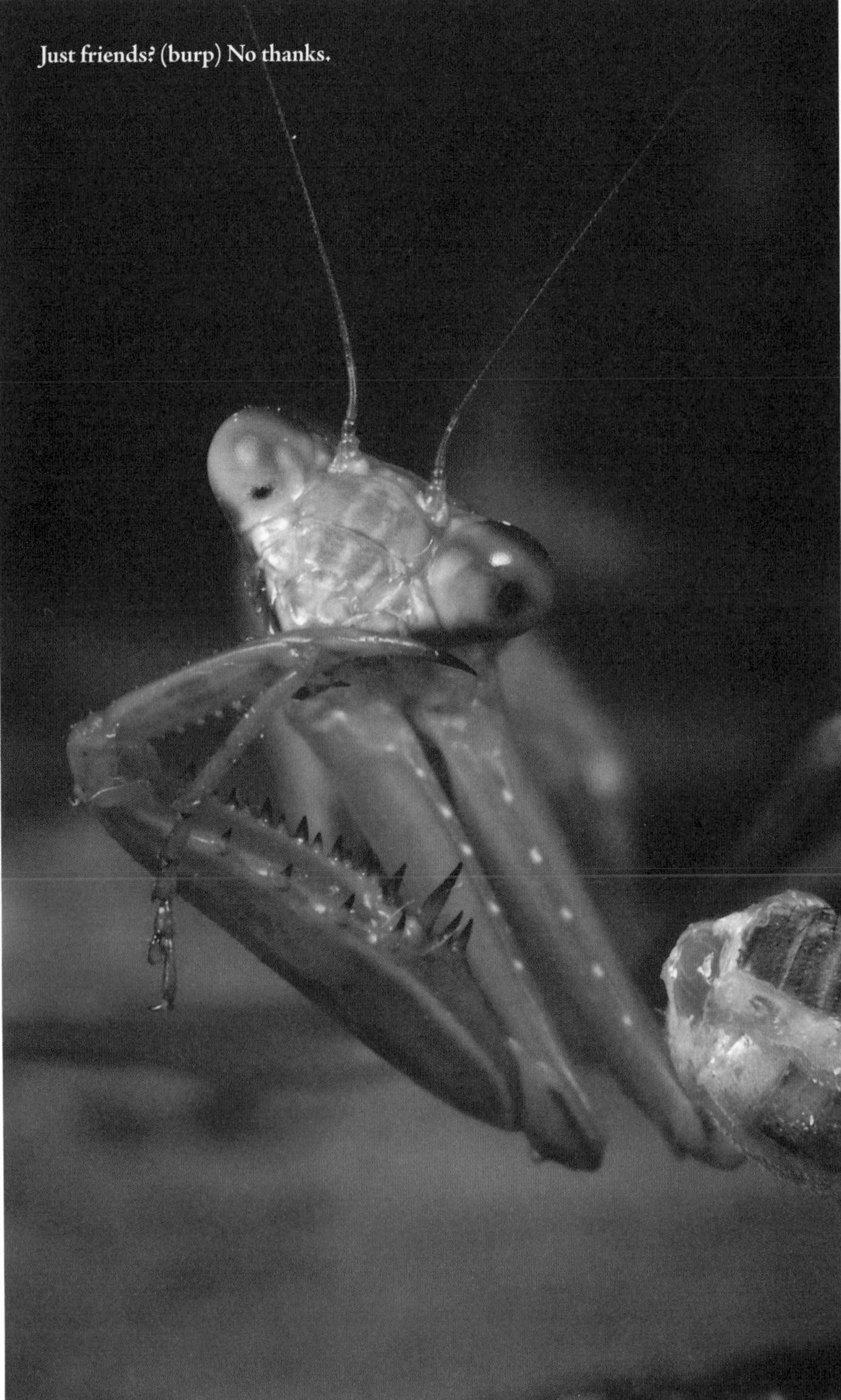
Just friends? (burp) No thanks.

How Being Just Friends Is a Waste of Time

"Day, n. A period of twenty-four hours, mostly misspent."

Ambrose Bierce

The Desperation of "Just Friends"

We both read and respond to dating questions on different online message boards like on www.marriable.com, and queries like this one are a dime a dozen:

"The dreaded four words"

I recently went out with this girl from work. We just went for coffee first, the second time to a singles event. I called her up for something more date-ish like dinner and a movie, and she hit me with the "let's just be friends" line. Does this mean it's all over? Couldn't she be just wanting to take it slow? I say this because she called me a few days later just to talk. She's too hard to read if she has any interest in dating me. What am I allowed to do as "just friends"? How do I get to know this girl and she me without wasting my time? The few times I brought it up she just avoided the subject. Help me, Obi-Wan Kenobi, you're my only hope!

Re: "The dreaded four words"

Oh, young Jedi, you are truly being tested by the Dark Side. When someone, *anyone* says, "let's just be friends," it's over. Besides, in your case it sounds like it didn't even get started. Sure, you had a couple casual activities with this girl, but when you suggested something "date-ish," she was *kind* enough to let you know you had no chance. Instead of torturing this girl who had your heart in mind when she said "no chance," let her be and move on. As for her phone calls, if they persist, be polite, keep them to less than three minutes, and interrupt the conversations to run to the thing you're "running late for" that day. She'll get the hint that you're not looking for more friends or desperate enough to hang out with her since you can't find any more prospects. And don't romanticize that she'll be even more drawn to you when you "play hard to get." That's just Desperate Vader talking . . . and he's not your father.

Now, you might have read this confused puppy's email and said, "How obvious, she doesn't dig him." But so many people make fools of themselves ignoring subtle signs like "I DON'T LIKE YOU LIKE THAT" to sail the river denial hoping the other will see the error of his or her ways.

Here are some of the signs you're wasting time being "just friends":

- You're waiting for the other person to "come around"
- Neither of you is into the other (that you know of)
- You've got no other options right now, so why not?

We can't say it any more plainly than this: if one of you doesn't have chemistry, you don't have chemistry as a couple. One of the dangers with male/female friendships is that more often than not one of the two wants something more from the relationship. In the end, usually either a heart is broken or, at the very least, the person with the crush is wasting time not looking elsewhere. If you are holding on to a long-term friendship in hopes that one day it will magically turn to love, you are lying to yourself. The chances that your friend will wake up one day and see you in a *totally different* and romantic light are miniscule. Save yourself the heartache. Keep friendship with the same sex and **save the opposite sex for love.**

Friendships Masquerading as Dating Relationships

Here are some more horror stories we've heard and what we had to say about them.

I have my eye on a certain guy at the volunteer center. We both work on projects together and spend a lot of time planning events, dreaming up possibilities, and stuff like that. We go out to eat at least once a week. He tells me all that's going on in his life. I mean, it's like we are dating but without the commitment or the holding hands or flirting or anything. I feel like we're dating, but the other day he said something about this girl that he likes, and it threw me for a loop. Why does he spend so much time with me if he's not into me? And why would he tell me about another girl when it's so obvious I like him? Shall I tell him how it makes me feel? Or just wait for him to talk about it?

—Mistaken for a Girlfriend

Dear Mistaken for a Girlfriend,

Oops, big mistake. Hanging out with a guy in hopes that he will one day get a clue and ask you out is a big lie. When a guy likes a girl, he doesn't let anything get in the way of dating her. Your girlfriends might say that it's really unfair of him to lead you on and spend so much time with you, but all he's guilty of is liking you enough to hang out but not enough to date. That's the lesson you've got to learn about guy/girl friendships: usually one of the two people has more feelings than the other, and they both end up lying to themselves about the situation in order to get what they want. You wanted time with the one you really liked

(loved?), and he liked being able to get all this girl worship for free until he found someone he really wanted to date. Don't lead yourself on any longer. If he hasn't asked you out by now, then he's not going to. You have to be honest with yourself and admit you are hanging on to nothing. If you don't want to get hurt anymore, walk away and spend more time at the center with female volunteers. Don't hurt yourself by being friends with a man you love but who will never return that love. It's self-destructive and self-deceptive.

—Michael

I'm a guy and have a girl friend who lives in the same building as me, and we hang out a lot. She calls or IMs me every day and tells me everything about her day. It makes me feel really close to her. We've been hanging out, doing lunch, dinner, talking, etc., for about two years, and yesterday she told me that she had a date with this new guy that just moved in next door. I was totally shocked. I thought that our friendship was working toward something. Where did I go wrong? Why would she do this to me?

—A Day Late and a Dollar Short

Dear Day Late and a Dollar Short,

Do *what* to you? Wait two years for you to get up the nerve to ask her out on a real date? I think she gave you too much time! Listen, it

Sure Signs a Guy Is Interested

- **He asks you out.**
- **He tells you he is interested.**
- **He calls you when he says he will (or close to it).**
- **He wants to be with you.**
- **No matter what else is going on in his life, he will do all he can to be with you.**

shouldn't take two years to decide if you want to ask a girl out. If she was that important to you, you should have made the move and advanced the relationship. As it stands, she probably just considered you another girlfriend she could dump all her emotions on until she found the love of her life. You could have saved yourself a lot of heartache by making a move a year and a half ago instead of continuing to lie to yourself that "these things take time." Women can't be put on hold until you are certain they are into you. You must strike while the iron is hot. Next time, don't try to protect yourself by being friends first; find out if she likes you by asking her out. The two-year friendship/breakup thing is nothing you want to experience again.

—Hayley

Sure Signs a Guy Isn't Interested

- He doesn't ask you out.
- He never tells you he's interested.
- He is too busy to do things (or too stressed, too worried, too hurt, too whatever).

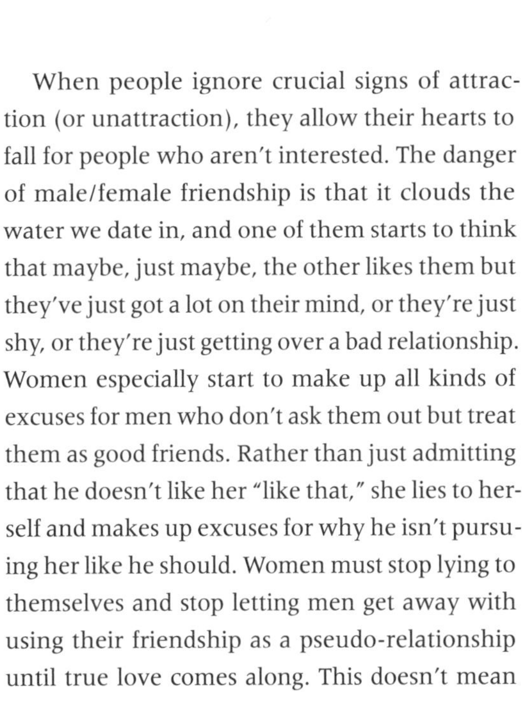

When people ignore crucial signs of attraction (or unattraction), they allow their hearts to fall for people who aren't interested. The danger of male/female friendship is that it clouds the water we date in, and one of them starts to think that maybe, just maybe, the other likes them but they've just got a lot on their mind, or they're just shy, or they're just getting over a bad relationship. Women especially start to make up all kinds of excuses for men who don't ask them out but treat them as good friends. Rather than just admitting that he doesn't like her "like that," she lies to herself and makes up excuses for why he isn't pursuing her like he should. Women must stop lying to themselves and stop letting men get away with using their friendship as a pseudo-relationship until true love comes along. This doesn't mean you have to run the other way when you see the just-friend male or female coming. Realize that you can be friendly without being friends.

Continued on page 84

Top 10 Rejection Lines Given by Women (And What They Actually Mean)

10. *I think of you as a brother.* (I don't want to kiss you, ever.)
9. *There's a slight difference in our ages.* (I'm not Mary Kay LeTourneau or Anna Nicole Smith.)
8. *I'm not attracted to you in that way.* (Again, I don't want to kiss you, ever.)
7. *My life is too complicated right now.* (Instead of "you complete me," you complicate me.)
6. *I've got a boyfriend.* (And his name is TiVo.)
5. *I don't date men where I work.* (And if you quit, I still work on Earth.)
4. *It's not you, it's me.* (It's me not wanting to date you.)
3. *I'm concentrating on my career.* (Until I find someone that I see a future with.)
2. *I'm celibate.* (How many times do I have to say it? I don't want to kiss you!)
1. *Let's be friends.* (You won't mind when I tell you about all the other men I meet and have a crush on, will you?)

Top 10 Rejection Lines Given by Men (And What They Actually Mean)

10. I THINK OF YOU AS A SISTER. (I'm just not attracted to you.)
9. THERE'S A SLIGHT DIFFERENCE IN OUR AGES. (I'm just not attracted to you.)
8. I'M NOT ATTRACTED TO YOU IN THAT WAY. (Um, what he said.)
7. MY LIFE IS TOO COMPLICATED RIGHT NOW. (I can't keep juggling you and dating my new crush.)
6. I'VE GOT A GIRLFRIEND. (I'm just not attracted to you enough to dump her.)
5. I DON'T DATE WOMEN WHERE I WORK. (I see a nasty breakup in our future, and I need this job.)
4. IT'S NOT YOU, IT'S ME. (It's you.)
3. I'M CONCENTRATING ON MY CAREER. (I'm just not attracted to you.)
2. I'M CELIBATE. (This is getting redundant . . .)
1. LET'S BE FRIENDS. (I value you as an important influence in my life and can't imagine navigating my free time without you being a part of it. Did I mention that I'm just not attracted to you?)

INSTANT MESSAGE from haze@marriable.com

Men need to read *Stand Up and Be a Man*, **page 109**.

Think that is too harsh? Then consider this: what happens when he gets a girlfriend, this guy friend of yours? It's pretty safe to bet that the new girl isn't going to want her man hanging out with another woman. You can plan to see time with him diminish and your status as "best friends" be lost forever. Don't put all your eggs in some other Jane Doe's basket.

Turning Desperate into *Marriable*

A lot of people might be screaming right now, "That's not right! Guys and girls can be friends, even after they're married." You can't be that naive! Come on, think about it. You've found the love of your life. You have a beautiful courtship, you go on an amazing honeymoon, you move into your dream house, and two weeks later your spouse tells you they are going to dinner with their best friend, who happens to be of the opposite sex. How does that make you feel? No problem, you say? Then think about the idea that every time you have a fight, your spouse will be calling their "best friend" to complain about you. And that best friend, at that point, is going to seem really great. Better than you, even. The chance that your mate could fall into an adulterous affair with their "best friend" of the opposite sex is nothing to flirt with. The reality is that once you are married, having a friend of the opposite sex isn't appropriate. Just consider that as you put all your friendship eggs into the basket of the opposite sex.

WARNING
(CONTENT BLOCKED):
This page contains adult material and has
been blocked by your service provider.
(CONTENT BLOCKED):
This page contains adult material and has
WARNING
WARNING
(CONTENT BLOCKED):
This page contains adult material and has
been blocked by your service provider.
(CONTENT BLOCKED):
WARNING
(CONTENT BLOCKED):
This page contains adult material and has
been blocked by your service provider.
(CONTENT BLOCKED):
WARNING
(CONTENT BLOCKED):
WARNING
(CONTENT BLOCKED):
This page contains adult material and has
been blocked by your service provider.

Male Porn Makes You Desperate

> The porn industry is a $57 billion worldwide business.

> "Porn revenue is larger than all combined revenues of all professional football, baseball and basketball franchises."[2]

If you're a guy and you're looking at porn, you're not *Marriable*, period. Pornography makes you desperate. Desperate for a life you're not living. So desperate, in fact, that you actually believe the lie that people live that kind of life and are happy. For purposes of discussion, male porn will be defined here as whatever puts a tingle in your jingle. Typically this consists of skin.

Any experience of arousal can pump adrenaline. Viewing pornography can intensify this, and like any "high," your body will only crave more. This is why psychologists and counselors recognize the patterns of addiction and escalation. Beer commercials, sideline cheerleaders, and waitresses peddling buffalo wings in hot pants all can serve as an entree into male porn. And as those images lose their potency, guys will start to search for something more exciting. Dr. Victor Cline of the University of Utah lays out this progression in four steps:

Addiction: You keep coming back to porn. It becomes a regular part of your life. You're hooked and can't quit.

Escalation: You start to look for more graphic pornography. You start using porn that disgusted you earlier but is now enticing to you.

Desensitization: You begin feeling numb toward the images you see. Even the most graphic porn is no longer arousing. You become desperate to feel the same thrill again, but you can't find it.

Acting out sexually: This is the point when you make a critical jump and start acting out the images you have seen and rehearsed in your mind.[3]

Men's "lifestyle" magazines, pay-per-view movies in the privacy of your hotel

U.S. porn revenue exceeds the combined revenues of the ABC, CBS, and NBC television networks ($6.2 billion).[4]

Though the networks seem to be closing the gap in prime-time nudity.

My Porn Merit Badge

In seventh grade, I briefly attempted a stint in the Boy Scouts. The first night of my first weekend campout, four of my fellow scouts and I were enjoying the post-chili cookout noisemaking in our tent when my friend "Billy" whipped out some magazines from his backpack. Needless to say, they were eye-opening. In fact, I had no idea what I was looking at, I just knew it was wrong. Back then the only way you could be exposed to porn was if one of your friends had it, your dad had a stash under his bed, or you tried to buy it at a seedy mini-mart or adult bookstore.

Michael

A Woman's Point of View

When a woman is dating a guy who is looking at porn, it makes her feel like he's cheating on her. Is he really so weak and desperate for sex that he has to pretend he's getting it from some imaginary woman he'll never meet? Sorry, guys, but for most of us girls, it just makes you slimy. If you want to avoid looking desperate, avoid looking at porn. It's just plain ugly.

room, and the Internet have flooded our senses and provided ample opportunity to view all manner of skin. Even prime-time network TV has disclaimers for nudity and sexual content. This chapter is not going to explain why porn is wrong; plenty of books and articles deal with that subject. This section is going to deal with how porn affects your *Marriability*.

Okay, that about covers this chapter.

The more someone looks at porn, the more the person's senses become deadened sexually (and the greater appetite they have for images that go further than the last ones viewed). While one might think that porn can be compartmentalized in secret, married men who are honest will tell you that if you look at porn nightly, weekly, or even once every couple of months, chances are great that your wife will look less and less attractive to you. And we can all agree that can't be good for a marriage relationship.

The fact that male porn is a broad addiction is beautifully summed up in the titles of two best-selling books on the subject, *Every Man's Battle* by Steve Arterburn and *Men's Secret Wars* by Patrick Means. Instead of women turning a blind eye to "boys being boys," they need to consider this: while you're waiting for marriage before letting him in your bed, if the guy you're dating is looking at porn, he's cheating on you. He's seeing women and he can't say no.

For a guy, being *Marriable* means being willing to grow up and be a man and having a healthy view of marriage. That healthy view starts in his single life. Male porn has no place in a healthy marriage, so guys, kick the habit now.

"But I Like It Too"

Amazingly enough, more and more women are into male porn as a relationship-building tool. We'll leave it for good morally-based marital counselors to decide if this is good for these confused couples, but when women encourage men to watch porn or watch it themselves, they probably have a confidence or self-worth issue to address. Ladies, consider that what you are asking him to do is to begin to put into his mind images of other women who probably look a lot hotter than you. You are feeding his mind with warped images that will forever stain his memory, not to mention yours. Porn isn't just a play toy used to enhance your sexual high; it's an addictive element that brings another person, or a cast of people, into your bedroom.

Turning Desperate into *Marriable*

Inviting porn into a relationship simply points out how desperate you are for the next high. If someone has to rely on porn to get them off, then we know that before long they will need more and harder porn for that same high. Porn usage is simply a sign of someone who has done so much and gone so far that they need harder and harder images to get the job done. Watching porn makes you desperate in your need for the perfect sexual encounter, and it makes you desperate in your need for more and harder images. Don't get stuck in the desperate pit of porn.

You've Got Addiction X

"In my clinical practice, I have treated both children and adults who have been unequivocally and repeatedly injured by exposure to pornography. If anyone still has doubts about pornography's effects, I would suggest that he or she get invited to some meetings of 'Sexaholics Anonymous' and personally witness the pain and trauma first hand."

—Victor B. Cline, Ph.D.[5]

INSTANT MESSAGE
from bobismydog@marriable.com

For more info on kicking the porn habit, see www.marriable.com. ☹

WARNING (CONTENT BLOCKED):

This page contains adult material and has been blocked by your service provider.

WARNING (CONTENT BLOCK

This page contains adult material and has been blocked by your service provider.

WARNING (CONTENT BLOC

This page contains a been blocked by you

WARNING (CONTENT BLOCKED):

This page contains adult material and has been blocked by your service provider.

WARNING (CONTENT BLOCKED):

This page contains adult material and has been b

WARNING (CONTENT BLOCKED):

This page contains adult ma been blocked by your servic

WARNING (CONTENT BLOCKED):

This page contains adult material and has been blocked by your service provider.

Faa Mous Auuthoor

WARNING (CONTENT BLOCKED):

This page contains adult material and has been blocked by your service provider.

Female Porn: The Seedy Underbelly of Chick Flicks and Romance Novels

Just like male porn revs guys' engines in unhealthy ways, female porn is leading women astray. Let's embrace equality and take a closer look at the study of "what women want," exposing the desperate side of chick flicks and romance novels.

Each year hundreds of thousands of women whet their romantic appetites with enticing tales of perfect romance and fairy-tale endings. The romance parade starts as early as a parent is able to read to their little girl. Stories about princesses and the princes who rescue them from certain doom are read over and over and over again. While boys are busy building things and tearing them down again, or maybe reading a spy novel or horror story, little girls are dreaming of the perfect wedding and the dream house. As they mature, young women soon find more of an escape from reality in movies and novels. And when the Pottery Barn catalog arrives, they dream of how amazing their lives would be if only they had that couch and those throw pillows. The female psyche, how different it is from the males. And how desperate its distractions.

For decades the religious community has publicly condemned the pornographic industry as

Would You Mind If I Told You a Porn Story?

by Hayley

A few years ago I went to a movie with my roommate. The movie was *The Saint*, starring the once-sexy Val Kilmer. It was an adventure movie in the footsteps of James Bond. Murder, foreign intrigue, and, yes, romance. As the hero, Val, saved the world and the girl, we sighed. At the end of the movie, Val met his leading lady in the ultimate romantic cabin in the woods. The room was divine. Animal skin rugs adorned the floors; candles were the only light. Flower petals decorated the overstuffed bed, and she jumped into his arms as he carried her off for a night of romantic passion. As the credits rolled, my friend and I looked at each other and breathed deeply. We both bit our bottom lips and looked back to the screen as if hoping for just a little more. After all the credits had run and the lights came up in the theater, I turned and said to my friend, "I need a cold shower." She smiled and said, "So do I." Ah, chick flicks, they get the heart of a healthy woman a-racin'!

destructive to the sexual appetites of the men who indulge therein. Most people see that it creates a gap between the sexes. It nurtures the lie that women are something that they aren't, and in the end it harms real loving and nurturing relationships. Those airbrushed images are anything but real, let alone attainable.

Yet female pornography has for decades been an accepted pastime, sliding under the radar of the religious right and instead being promoted as an acceptable distraction from the worries of life. But what exactly is female porn? Is there a definition for this newly discovered blight on society? For the answer to this question, we need look no further than the honorable Mr. Webster and his infamous dictionary of words. How we overlooked this definition for years upon years we do not know. But we are here today to uncover the truth. To shed light in the dark. And so without further ado here it is:

> pornography – 3: the depiction of acts in a sensational manner so as to arouse a quick intense emotional reaction[6]

Catch that? *Emotional.* We contend that the job of the chick flick, romance novel, and love song is to arouse a quick, intense emotional reaction. Can you feel it? We ask you, ladies, what else arouses a stronger emotion in you than that heart-fluttering chick flick? What else gets you to dream of the perfect man and pray to God that you will get one *just like him*?

If you are using too many of these, you may be indulging in quick intense emotional reactions, or you may just have allergies.

Any attack on the traditional porn industry always includes the cry that it creates unrealistic expectations in men. No woman can be that hot and sexy all the time. It's just not fair to women for their men to look at that. (Of course there are other deep concerns, but we went into that in the last chapter.) However, the very thing that women complain about in male porn is also created by female porn.

Continued on page 98

Insert image for centerfold here.
Print one-sided, full-color, foldout, on glossy paper.
Saddle-stitch in center of book.

Check the pulse on any leading man from the biggest chick flicks and this is the rhythm his heart beats to: undying love, pure romance, sweet words, heroic rescues, persistent pursuit, tears, laughter, protection, flowers, gifts, and devotion. He never farts or burps. He's never grumpy or wanting to be left alone.

Michael,

Hey, there's no reason to single me out here.

Hayley,

Oh, honey, you are my night in farting armor.

He's always focused on the female, exhausting all his energies on pleasing her. He is the ultimate creation of the self-centered female who wants the world to revolve around her and her alone. Just as male porn caters to a man's physical desire to be pleased by his mate, so female porn offers the same self-absorbed emotional aphrodisiac.

Misery: The Ultimate Outcome of Female Pornocopia

The result of exposure to this kind of fairy tale is obvious, at least to us. When a single woman leaves a steamy chick flick only to return home alone to her cats and tub of ice cream, a part of her breaks—the heart part. And she feels more alone than ever.

Hayley,

Yes, I had cats, and yes, I know that of which I speak.

The man was hers, but only for two and a half hours, and now, like every other man, he's gone.

The same kind of letdown happens every time the newest home decor catalog comes to the house. She looks over all of the latest home fashions and then looks around her house. Suddenly a sense of "I'm just not good enough" overcomes her. And she senses an insatiable urge to purchase a new antiqued armoire and festive dish set.

Turning Desperate into *Marriable*

Romance is a decidedly desirable component of dating. Women love it. Guys know it, girls know it, the American people know it. Guys who are consistently adept at providing a chick-flick feel to their dates tend to have more success getting and keeping a girl interested. And no question, guys can take lessons from the movies for creative ideas. But when it comes down to it, because of an addiction to female porn, women can easily cast in their minds leading men with no flaws, shortcomings, or insecurities. The Good Book says to "guard our hearts."[7] If the number of romance novels and chick flicks you consume in a month exceeds the number of dates on your social calendar, you may be getting out of balance.

Plain and simple, the more you live in reality, understanding and accepting the good and the bad of the opposite sex, the less desperate and more *Marriable* you become.

Hayley,

Ah, the subtle affects of female porn—leaving us alone again (without a leading man), overweight (because of the ice cream), and broke (from the shopping spree).

Michael,

But at least you have twenty new throw pillows to fill that empty space next to you on the couch. Why *do* you women buy so many pillows?

You complete me.

Don't Marry Your Best Friend Unless You're Gay

> Marriage is an alliance entered into by a man who can't sleep with the window shut and a woman who can't sleep with the window open.
>
> George Bernard Shaw

> I love being married. It's so great to find that one special person you want to annoy for the rest of your life.
>
> Rita Rudner

You've heard it a thousand times, maybe even murmured it yourself in zombie-like agreement: "I want to marry my best friend." While it sounds completely logical at first, allow us to make some observations about the best friend spouse myth. If you're like most, you've grown up having best friends of the same sex. For ease of explanation, let's use sweeping stereotypes (plus, they're so much more fun!).

Male Bonding: Attendance Is 100 Percent of the Grade

At the core of man-to-man relationships is the simple question, "Did both guys show up?" When guys have other guys as best friends, they are defined by the number and types of activities they participate in. This means that if you're a guy, your best friends historically have been those who have done things with you like sports, blowing things up, making creative noises with your bodies, doing semi-illegal things with automobiles, and snapping towels at each other in the locker room. For instance, picking another guy up from the airport or helping him move is a telltale sign of a budding best friend. And during these activities, guys have the option of hardly speaking without any danger of offending the other guy.

Female Friend Grading: Class Participation and Book Reports

Girls, on the other hand, will quantify their best friends not by the activities they do together but rather by the following formula: take the sum of the sheer numbers of words, hopes, fears, and tears exchanged with one another and multiply by the frequency of contact. This phenomenon is known scientifically as *nonstopus talkus lottimus*. And when it comes to words, make no mistake, girls want quality *and* quantity. But if they must, they'll begrudgingly settle for just quantity. So while guys key in on the activity or simply being in the presence of their friend to establish best buddyhood, girls care less about where they are with their galpal and focus on the quality of the sharing and quantity of conversation.

A Crippling New Disease

Now, some of you may be saying, "But book-writer people, I've always had best friends of the opposite sex, so I'll be totally set when I meet my dream man/woman!" That just may be. But one key *Marriable* factor to consider when dating someone is how that person makes friends with the members of their own gender. Does she have lots of girlfriends, or does she just like to hang with the guys? Does he spend time with other guys who respect him as a man, or is he constantly trying to be chummy with the ladies? There is a name for this condition: ***Imbalanced Gender Friender Syndrome*** (IGFS).

IGFS is an insidious self-inflicted disease that is most prevalent in women but increasingly found in men. This typically occurs when girls decide other girls are too catty, too conniving, or just plain unsafe. So the girl afflicted with IGFS decides to cultivate friendships with the typically less emotional gender (see Hayley's book *Mean Girls: All Grown Up* for more).

Catty Women Alert
X
To rid yourself of this virus, please run MeanGirlsAGU.exe
MEAN
girls
all grown up
surviving catty and conniving women
Hayley DiMarco

While less common in men, IGFS can strike males with tremendous force, affecting males who are single-minded (no pun intended) on finding a woman to date and marry. This drive for companionship is so focused that the IGFS male usually sacrifices developing quality man-to-man relationships for increasing his face time with women. Many times this will even include cutthroat behavior like pursuing a girl that one of his guy "friends" is already chasing. This is a clear violation of the Guy Code. Other times this imbalance strikes when guys are so sensitive, deep, complex, and so on that hanging out with the boys and watching a game or going out for pizza with buddies from work is too shallow and lacks meaning.

Michael,

What? How can *pizza* lack *meaning*?

Hayley,

Spoken like a true man. Are there any vegetables on this pizza that answers the meaning of life?

Michael,

Does sauce count?

Dangerous Side Effects

While survival instincts usually trigger IGFS, side effects for the female sufferer include gradual loss of femininity, women constantly seeing you as a threat to steal their men, and the urge to belch in public. If—and we stress *if*—the IGFS female gets a man to "understand" her all-male friend revue while dating, serious shock waves are typically to come. Once engaged and married, fiancés and newlywed husbands have a difficult time understanding why their betrothed is going to the gym and then to lunch with her best friend Steve (who knows her so much better than her new hubby). Not only is this an extremely uncomfortable situation for the hubby, but it's extremely fertile ground for infidelity to take seed. Two possible scenarios emerge: fights in the marriage or loneliness for the female-friend-less wife. Ergo, the best-friend patterns for both the male and female of the species before marriage are set—set to be completely dysfunctional.

But what about having healthy men-to-men friendships and women-to-women friendships after marriage? When you marry someone of the opposite sex, that person is your new best friend, right? What if one or both parties desire the other as a best friend spouse, or *Besfrouse* as we like to

call them? Is becoming a Besfrouse achievable? Sure. Is it easy? Rarely. It's hard enough even to pronounce. Is it desirable? Only you and your potential Besfrouse can make that call.

Hayley,

Boy, can I relate. Half of my friends were men when I got engaged. And I must say that over the time of our engagement, I lost half of my friends. It just didn't seem cool to go out with single men after being married. And it hurt. They were true friends, but I had to choose between love and friendship, and I chose love!

Michael,

Plus, there's just something twisted about you hanging out with me and one of my "girl friends" when she knows me better than you. When I'm so used to sharing all my feelings with her, guess who I'll go to when we're having problems?

Hayley,

Yuck! Gimme that black book . . .

Ask yourself this question: "How many best friends have I had in my life so far?" Most would surely answer more than one (we would). Why is this? Because your best friend in third grade moved out of state, your best friend in middle school became a pothead, and your best friend in tenth grade tried out for soccer when you ran for student council and you started hanging out in different crowds. The point is, most people change best friends when it suits them.

Besides the confusing fact that your best friend has historically been the same sex as you, other factors can mess up a marriage where one or both partners think their mate has to be their best bud. Best friends come and best friends go, and it's usually because of disagreements, fights, or just moving apart. We get used to new best friends replacing old best friends when those old best friends wear out on us or grow apart from us. And so we get into this pattern that if you're going to be my best friend, then you'd better be on my side all the time, agree with me most of the time, be going the same direction as me, have the same interests as me—the list of requirements goes on and on. But what happens when your Besfrouse drifts apart from you and you no longer feel like best friends? Is it a sign the marriage is over? Do you pack up and move on to the next Besfrouse? Society has just the remedy for what ails your marriage if you're living with someone who's no longer your best friend but merely your spouse. It's called *no-fault divorce.* You see, you used to need a "good reason" for divorce, like adultery. We often hear, "But how do I know for sure that I married my true soul mate? Maybe I made a mistake!" To that we ask, "Did you say 'I do'? Did they?" If you both did, then guess what? *You married the one*. Once you've said I do, that's it, guessing over. It's time for people to stop looking for their best friend in their husband or wife and start seeing them as their husband or wife for life.

INSTANT MESSAGE
from haze@marriable.com

Also see *Marriable vs. Divorceable*, **page 171.**

Turning from Desperate to *Marriable*

The main reason we're rejecting the marrying your best friend theory is that it's basically a bad analogy. In marriage a couple doesn't always get along. They don't always agree. They drift apart, they drift back, but they never say, "You don't feel like my best friend anymore, so I'm finding a new one." When you say, "I'm going to marry my best friend," you'll also start measuring your dating relationships against this false standard. You expect your "other" to fill the same roles your friends are supposed to instead of auditioning them for the role of your husband or wife. Determining your compatibility is serious business, and you shouldn't feel an unnecessary burden of worrying "how is this going to affect our friendship?" Dating is not about finding friends; it's about finding a mate. Remember that you're trying out love interests like any other interest—try ice skating for a couple months and never touch your skates again, or join a hockey league so you play all year long. Dating is about trying people out to see if you belong together. Having this perspective gives you freedom from desperation and freedom from the friendship myth, which lets you weed out the time wasters so you can move on to finding "the one."

Marriage is not all about friendship. It's a commitment to stay together even when you don't *feel* like best friends or have any romantic emotions. It's about sharing the rest of your life, good and bad, not just having a good time. You lose the option of changing partners, but you'll gain all the other greater benefits of marriage.

Having a realistic and accurate view of what friendships are for (being friends) and what dating is for (finding a mate) will help you navigate the waters of your social life and increase your chances of recognizing a person who's just as *Marriable* as you.

ALERT! X

Your Marriable Definition Is Out of Date.

The concept of marriage is something totally unique.

It's not friendship.

It's not having a girlfriend/boyfriend.

It's not a business partnership.

It's not playing doubles in tennis (even though all matches start with love).

You can walk away from a friend for any reason. You date girlfriends/boyfriends to learn what you like and need in a mate. You can dissolve a business partnership, void contracts, and execute escape clauses. You can even dump your doubles partner because his doughnut addiction keeps him from attacking the net. But marriage was designed to be different. A spouse is supposed to do something that no other role does: stay and work it out. Till death do you part. In sickness and in health. For richer or poorer. No excuses.

Just give me a minute, will you!

Stand Up and Be a Man

> The real man smiles in trouble, gathers strength from distress, and grows brave by reflection.
>
> Thomas Paine

> The successful man is the average man, focused.
>
> Anonymous

Send in the Clowns

Women are forever asking, "Where have all the real men gone?" They feel as if they are surrounded by a lot of scared, quiet, sweet men who just aren't willing to step up to the plate, sweep them off their feet, and ride off into the sunset. Nice guys abound, but where are the real men?

The answer, ladies: You asked them to act more like women. To be sensitive, talkative, caring, sharing, and sweet. And now that you've got your wish, you yearn for the good old days when men were men and women were women. We can hardly blame men for abandoning their masculine ways when neutering women scream at them, "I'm strong enough to open my own door, thank you very much!"

Face it, ladies, men are confused.

Do you want them to be feminine or masculine? Do you want them to sweep you off your feet or to follow your lead? Where are the real men, you ask? They are lost in a state of confusion. "What do women want?" they plead. "Do you want a man's man or a girly man?"

In women's attempts to get more of what they want—communication, sensitivity, and attention—they've thrown away a lot more of what they had that wasn't so bad. Men and women alike need to make up their minds. What will it be, masculinity or femininity? Maybe women want both in a man, but that experiment hasn't proved that successful. Sure, some men may be able to masterfully balance their strong masculinity with a feminine side of sharing, caring, shopping, and cooking with their woman, but most men only end up confused puppies as they try to master two completely different approaches to life.

Any thorough examination of nature and the history of man would show that for whatever reason, God created men and women to be different. He gave men certain skills and abilities that served the community, while he gave women others that equally but differently served the same community. We can easily imagine how incomplete we would be as a species if we all were programmed or designed to think and act the same way. It would be like having a body that was all eyes and arms and no feet or legs. The body works so well because of the varying responsibilities and strengths of each body part, and society works just the same way. The male psyche has something very important to contribute to the female

Ladies, Enjoy the Man in Your Man

A lot of women complain that their men just don't talk enough. They whine over the fact that he doesn't share his feelings. And to that I say, *Congratulations, you have yourself a man.* Would you rather he be a woman? Every time the man in your life acts like—ugh!—such a man, say a prayer of thanks. Thank God that he *is* a man. With that comes good and annoying qualities, but you can't hate one while loving the other. Enjoy the complete package. The next time he is "such a man," give him a big hug and tell him you love his masculinity.

psyche, and any rush to demasculinize a man is a surefire recipe for disaster.

When a woman asks, "Where have all the real men gone?" what is she really asking? What traits in a man is she longing for? She is certainly not saying, "I wish I could find a guy who was more sensitive" or "Where are all the nice guys?" More than likely what she is longing for is a masculinity that draws out her own femininity and allows her to feel cared for and protected. Some women might be reading this and saying, "Wait! I can do everything a man can do!" Well, then, why do you want to get married? You can be able to do everything he can do and still want him to do it anyway. A woman who allows a man to do the things he is good at becomes so much more *Marriable*. So we're not saying you shouldn't be able to do the things you are able to do. Just give him a break and let him do some man things. If a woman is looking for "a real man," then she has to allow him to be "a real man."

And guys, before you start feeling like you're off the hook and it's all the woman's fault, think again. It takes two to dance this desperate tango. You have some things of your own you've got to get control of.

Real Men Know When to Chase

Sure, guys, you get a stroke to your ego when a woman asks you out. But the truth is, when you sit back and wait for her to ask, you have just led her to ask herself, "Where have all the real men gone?" Many women think they have the right to ask a man out, but when she *has* to ask him out, somewhere deep inside she is thinking, *Why doesn't this guy have the guts to ask me out himself?* And when she asks, the entire order of things starts shifting. If she asks, then she pays. But if she pays, does she pick you up? Does she get you at your front door? Where does it end—when she carries you over the threshold? When do you become the man so she gets back to being the girl—when she gets pregnant? It won't work. So take back your manhood and find a woman to ask out. Not sure how to find a willing woman? Let us help.

Hayley,

The truth is, guys, that every woman, whether she will admit it or not right now, wants to be chased. It's as ancient as Cinderella and Sleeping Beauty. Women have a deep desire to be found so beautiful that men would search the ends of the earth for them, fight for them, and yes, even risk rejection for them. Nothing is more attractive to a woman than the man she's interested in being sure enough of himself to ask her out.

Michael,

And really, nothing is more fun. We're a competitive bunch and love being the hero. Comic books, westerns, and action movies are in our blood. Defeat evil *and* get the girl—that's what we're all about.

Here's some help on when to ask and when not to bother. (Girls, if you don't know these tricks and you're tempted to go straight to calling him, try some of these flirting techniques on him and he's much more likely to pick up the phone.)

The best way to get a yes if you are deathly afraid of rejection is to try flirting first. Flirting helps you take the risk out of asking her out.

When you flirt with her and she flirts back (don't skip that part—"she flirts back"!), you can have more confidence that she won't reject you. So before you ask a woman out, hedge your bets. Find out a few things about your chemistry before you dive nose-first into an empty pool. A woman will give you signs that she is interested (if she's smart). This will give you, the man, permission to ask her out and a certain degree of certainty that she won't reject you. It's called flirting, and used wisely, it saves the world a lot of heartache. If you really watch the woman you are interested in and make your presence known, she should give you all the signals you need.

The biggest sign is body language. What is she saying with her body that she's not saying with her lips? Here are some things she might be doing that are a sure sign she's interested. If she's interested she:

- stands a little straighter when you walk by. Something about attracting men makes women want to stand up a little straighter. Maybe it's a primal way of showing you her body, but whatever the reason, it can be a sign she's noticed you and she's interested. Or that she has a back brace from her fender bender. In that case, always offer to drive.
- looks you in the eye and then maybe looks away quickly, followed by the "lookback." This is a stereotypical flirt technique, and it sends signals like nothing else. Just make sure she isn't sneaking looks in disbelief at your latest facial piercings.

- talks to you. Most women who like you will at least make an attempt to talk to you. Remember, women love to talk, and she needs to find out if you're suitable for her conversation style—witty, deep, political, nonstop, or whatever.
- touches her hair a lot or does the fail-safe laugh and hairflip. It's seductive, it's feminine, and it often means come a little closer.
- moves like you. If your hand is on your face, she moves her hand to her face. For some reason, when we are interested in someone, we tend to agree with our bodies. Ah, bodygreement.
- touches you lightly, usually on the shoulder or forearm. This minor invasion of your personal space is generally done only by women who want to know you more. If she has made no effort to touch you, then she might not want you touching her.
- compliments you. Seldom will a woman compliment a guy she isn't into. So watch out for those oh-so-sweet compliments.

If you aren't seeing any of these signals, then you either have a shy girl or an uninterested girl, so here's how to probe a little more without risking major rejection.

The main thing in chasing a woman is that you don't wait for her to make the first move. Flirting can really help you know if the chances are good that she will say yes, but you are the one who has to risk all and ask—that is, start the chase.

When you really like a woman and want to ask her out, you need to get the signals going. Asking someone out cold turkey is kind of a shock to the system. First she needs to see that you are interested and be allowed to show you that she is interested as well. So slow the boat down and try some of these things before you dive in and ask her to do something with you.

Notice her—Women love to be noticed. It makes them feel great. So make sure she sees you seeing her. Don't act like some kind of construction worker on break, but do sneak a peek at her so she catches you.

Look her in the eyes—If you can't look a woman in the eyes, you can't get her attention. Women are all about eyes; they love 'em, and they love it when you look them in the eye. But don't overdo it—the stalker stare will send her walking, er, running for cover.

Be clean and smell good—Smells don't really matter to men, but for some reason, women find them really important. They get turned on by what they smell, so why not give her what she wants? Brush your teeth, shower regularly, check your breath, and, yes, keep your breath strips handy.

Try to get to know her—Women want to be known. They want someone to really get who they are. So ask her about herself, let her talk, let her express herself. The more she can tell you about herself, the more she'll like you.

Show that you are attracted—Women need clues just like you do. They need to know you are interested. At this point, a comment like "Wow, you look great!" will work and still prevent you from

Michael,

Are you going to tell them?

Hayley,

That you smell like my dad? Ah yes, it's true. There's something comforting and protective about it. If a woman still has a little girl crush on her dad, a guy who smells like dad has a secret advantage.

Michael,

I can literally hear guys running to the store to buy Aqua Velva and Old Spice right now.

getting sued for sexual harassment. Then in turn they will let you know they are attracted by some of the previously mentioned tells (to use a poker term). And *bam!* asking her out is a go! Show her you are attracted and see how she reacts. If she is obviously cold, then she's probably not interested, so don't risk rejection or the aforementioned lawsuit. But if she responds positively, then dive in.

Smile at her—A smile speaks a thousand words. And it can even be kind of sexy, especially when you don't talk a bunch but smile from across the room. It's mystery with obvious attraction. Smiling works (unless combined with the stalker stare . . . eewww).

Be where she is—Find out what she likes and what she does and show up there. Now, don't become a stalker guy; everything in moderation. If she obviously couldn't care less that you are there, then back off. Don't push yourself on her, but if she shows signs of liking you, you can continue to be where she is.

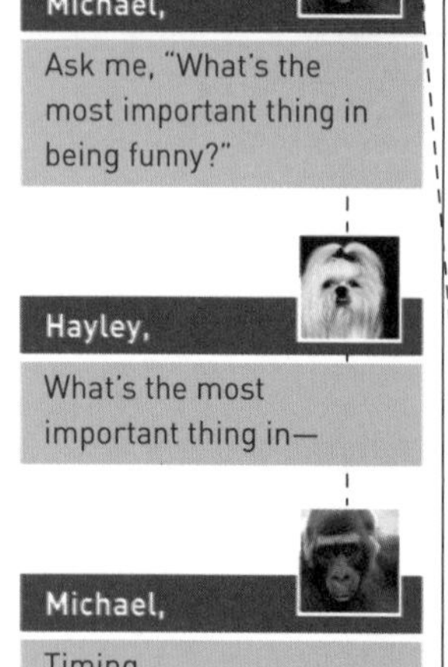

Michael,
Ask me, "What's the most important thing in being funny?"
Hayley,
What's the most important thing in—
Michael,
Timing.

Give her compliments—Compliments go a long way. A lot of girls don't know how to take a compliment, but that doesn't mean you should stop giving them. Compliments need to be founded in truth, though. Don't make stuff up; you really gotta mean it.

Say something funny—Women often say humor is the most important thing in a man. So don't take yourself too seriously, even if you aren't a comedian. Crack a joke; it's safer than asking her out cold turkey. Check out her response. If she laughs, chances are much better that she's interested. If she just looks at you like you're a freak, probably not a safe bet to ask her out.

Stand tall—Don't stand all hunched over; women like a man who stands up and gets noticed. It shows your confidence.

Touch her a little—Touch her lightly on the back, shoulders, or arm when you help her put her coat on, get the door for her, or guide her across the street. Don't get all gropey, though, or you'll blow the whole thing. This is more of a first or second date thing, unless you've been doing the "friends" thing awhile and you're trying to see if you can salvage the possibility of love from the dismal depths of being "just friends."

Once you get the signals going, if she's given you any kind of clue that she's interested, then step up to the plate and ask her out. Don't ask a group of people *and* her—be a man and ask her out one-on-one. She'll love you for it. Of course, if she says no, then assess the situation. If she really seems to have something else to do, try for another date. But if you have a sense she just doesn't want to go out with you, then lay off. If you keep asking her, you will look desperate to her and every other girl who's watching.

INSTANT MESSAGE
from bobismydog@marriable.com

See *How Being Just Friends Is a Waste of Time*, **page 75**

If you still are afraid of the chase, then consider this. What if we were to give you an endless supply

Continued on page 120

Chasing Your Girlfriend

Once you've got the ball rolling and you've got a couple of dates under your belt, don't give up on the chasing thing. She still needs to know she's the prey and you're the hunter. Here are some things you both need to know when it comes to the relationship.

The man calls more—When it comes to phone calls, the man should be the one making most of them. Sure, after you have been going out for a while, the woman can do some of the calling. But the man should keep things interesting by making most of the effort, i.e., chasing. If she's smart, she won't return *every* phone call. If she did, you might start to think she's too easy to get ahold of. The chase is more exciting when you think there's a possibility you might lose.

The man defines the relationship—Women love to talk, and they love to define things, but when they do, they take the reins away from men. If she's smart, she'll let you monitor things, and when you think it's time, you are the one who defines the relationship. It's part of the chase thing. The prey doesn't tell the hunter what's going to happen next.

The man gives more—For a woman, affection is largely related to things she gets. It's not that all women are greedy, it's just that cards, flowers, notes, and even attention mean a lot to a woman. Give her thoughtful things now and then and she'll feel loved. Overdo it and you'll look desperate. And avoid the whole one-month, two-month, three-month anniversary trap. This is setting you up to fail if you ever stop exercising your romance muscle. Give gifts when they aren't expected.

How to Ask a Woman Out

When asking a woman out on a date, consider the following:

Ask her out for a specific event – Don't say, "Hey, we should go out sometime" or "You wanna do something?" Ask for what you want! "Would you like to go out to dinner next Friday night, say 7:00?" or "Hey, I've got two tickets to 'Scooby on Ice'—they turn the zamboni into the Mystery Machine. It's so cool!—would you like to go next Saturday?"

Don't ask her when a bunch of people are around – This is more for your protection than for hers. If she says no, you will have saved yourself a lot of embarrassment by not asking her in front of the entire office.

If she says no, don't ask why – Just say, "Okay, maybe another time," and walk away. If she wants to go out with you, she will give you another date that works, or she may just start flirting with you more.

Never ask her more than twice – If she says no two times in a row, she probably means no forever, unless she also tells you that she "would *love* to but can't this weekend, so how about next weekend?" You don't want to be a pseudo-stalker, but you also need to make sure she isn't just really busy. That's always a possibility.

ASK HER YOURSELF – DON'T ASK YOUR FRIEND TO FIND OUT IF SHE WILL DATE YOU. WHAT IS THIS, MIDDLE SCHOOL?

Ask her out for one date at a time – Don't get greedy and ask her out for several dates at once. Women like a bit of mystery in their men. When you are all over her too soon, it's a real turn-off.

Be direct – Say, "Would you like to . . . ?" Avoid things like, "I know you are busy, but I was wondering if maybe one day you might wanna . . ." Get to the point and get to it fast. Don't be a wimp. Know what you want and be direct.

The Man of My Dreams

by Hayley

I was always so impressed with Michael when we were dating because he had everything under control. He always knew how to get where we were going; we never got lost. He always had cash for tipping and change for the parking meter; he always made reservations. I felt like he was James Bond or something, because nothing surprised him. He was always the guy in charge. I could always trust that we were safe and in the right place. It was such a great feeling not to have to be the one in the know, not to have to be in charge for once. It really let me relax and let my hair down. I was allowed to enjoy my femininity rather than having to "be the man," as I was so accustomed to doing in other dating relationships.

of $1 bills with which you could buy lottery tickets at no risk to you? And say we guaranteed that in your lifetime, one of those dollars would hit the jackpot. Wouldn't you be laying those greenbacks down in a heartbeat, knowing your time was going to come? Trust us, we're not encouraging gambling or settling your retirement account with lotto tickets, but really, that's the type of control you have over your dating life. You have an endless supply of date invitations to offer—all you have to do is spend them. So get out there and start asking. It's the only manly thing to do.

Real Men Have a Plan

If you've ever played or followed sports, you know every team has a game plan. You need to be a man with a plan. You don't have to know exactly what's going to happen play by play, but you still have to do your preparation for game day. The same goes for the date. Nothing is worse for a woman than going out with a guy who has nothing planned. "What do you wanna do?" "I don't care. What do you wanna do?" is not a good opening conversation. You don't have to have a minute-by-minute schedule of events, but you need a general idea of what's going to happen so that she doesn't have to do the heavy lifting.

Plan before your date so you're not asking her to "go do something with you someday." Have a specific plan in mind when you ask her: "Hey, would you like to go to the park this weekend? They are doing Shakespeare in the Park on Saturday, and I hear it's pretty good." When you ask her out for a specific thing, you take the responsibility as to what you will do together on your date firmly out of her hands and free her up to spend her time daydreaming about how much fun you'll have and poring over all her outfits to find the perfect thing for Shakespeare in the Park.

Exception to the Plan: Of course, once you have a plan, you'll have to be ready and willing to alter it. Don't be so hardheaded and unwilling to go with the flow that you lose your date. If you wanted to go to a ball game but she has a headache and the crowd noise would kill her, be ready and willing to move on to something else.

Preplanning

The thing that makes her melt is when you are subtly in control. This isn't a loud, bossy kind of control; this is a man in control of his surroundings. Most women love the feeling of being pampered and cared for, and nothing screams care more than a man who has things taken care of. So if you are going to the opening night of a new movie, get the tickets in advance so it won't be sold out before you can get your tickets. You can even log on to movie websites and print your tickets from home if you can't get to the box office. Or if you are trying out a new restaurant, call and make reservations a few days before. Plans take you from just another guy to *wow, what a guy!*

A Planner Isn't a Dictator

Plans can be changed, as we've stated before. Be flexible. The best approach is to tell her what you have planned and then ask her how that sounds. If she frowns or squirms or just says "yuck," don't get upset. Have a plan B. But if she is forever whining about what you are doing, don't get discouraged; consider it insight into this girl's mind. She might not be the one for you. After all, who wants to be with a complainer? She needs to be gracious enough to go with you on your plans most of the time. Look at this as a good test of her character. Does she go with the flow or try to manipulate and control everything in her world? That's the beauty of being a man early on. An important part of dating is finding out if this person is the one you want to spend the rest of your life with. And if you want to spend the rest of your life as a man, then you probably want to find a woman who is comfortable with that.

Real Men Pay

The rule is, the one who asks, pays. And since you are the man and doing the asking, guess what? You'd better be prepared to pay. If you aren't, a woman will complain about you to her friends for weeks. You will become the brunt of all their jokes if you ask her to pay on the first date or even the second date. Nothing screams wimp more than

Still a dyed-in-the-wool "Let's go Dutch" dater?

Think about it like this. Your boss asks you to go out to lunch with him. You are superexcited. You load up in his BMW and head out to the hottest new spot in town. The lunch is great; you talk about the new project you are working on. You get lots of work done. When the huge bill comes, he looks at it and says to you, "Your half is $35.45." Would you lose a little respect for him? I mean, he invited you. You might not even have any cash on you, and if you had known it was going to cost you, you wouldn't have gone. Now think how she feels when you ask her to "go Dutch."

Does the Guy *Always* Have to Pay?

The general rule to live by is that if you are new to dating someone (you decide what new is), **you should never ask her to pay**. But as the relationship progresses and you start to see more of each other, you can expect her to occasionally offer to pay. Asking her to pay could still be a real turn-off to her, even later on in the relationship. But most women will always ask if they can't pay part or all of the expenses for a particular date. Early on, refuse, but as things get more and more serious, you can start to take her up on it.

The same goes for you **planning the dates.** This is highly recommended early on in the relationship, but of course we know you can't play cruise director your entire life. As you start to spend more and more time with each other, she will have plenty of ideas about what she would like to do. Of course, never get so lazy that you stop planning all together. That's when she starts to say things like, "The romance is gone."

MikesNotes (distant cousin to Cliff)—quick, concise, abbreviated, pithy summary of the text you just read:

YES! Guys should always pay except for the exceptions.

a man who won't pay. In fact, if you ask her to pay or to go Dutch, then you might as well have started the date with the words, "I only want to be friends" or "Dating me is going to be a drain on your purse, count on it." Because that's what asking her to open up her wallet means.

In doing research for this book, we heard the story of a guy who apparently didn't mean to ask the girl to pay but "forgot his wallet in the car," so he asked her to take care of it. *Loser! Run out to the car!* This makes you a loser not only in the game of love but also in the game of life. A man who asks a girl out and asks her to pay lacks character. Don't expect him to find true love any time soon.

The equality-seeking guy might not think that asking a woman to pay could make him look desperate, but oddly enough, it does. Compared to the "plan and pay man," the "Let's go Dutch" boy paints the picture that he obviously hasn't had a lot of successful dates. The woman instinctually knows this, and though she might feel a bit of disgust for him, she also might temper that with a bit of pity. Ah, the perfect recipe for eternal bliss!

This is a typical car door.

Don't even think about using this to pick her up without a tetanus shot kit.

This car door is an exception since it will probably open itself for her.

Real Men Are Real Gentlemen

When you pay for the date, you are paying only for the date, not the girl. In other words, just because you paid doesn't mean she owes you anything! A lot of guys get upset when they dole out a ton of dough on a woman and get no physical payoff in return. In fact, some women even have a sense that if he spends a lot of money, she somehow owes him something. But nothing could be further from the truth. News flash: prostitution is illegal in 49 of 50 states in the U.S. You aren't paying for anything but the pleasure of her presence and the opportunity to eventually either marry her or cross her off your list. When you expect any kind of physical payoff, you look desperate. You look like you can get action only when you pay for it. Again, women can sense if that's your motivation, and it's ugly to them! The *Marriable* guy doesn't need to shower a woman with gifts in order to connect with her on a physical level. He knows

Survey
X
Do You Think a Man Should Pay for Dinner?
1. Yes, always
2. It depends if I like him
3. Sometimes
4. No, both should share the cost
5. No, the girl should pay
6. Only if it's expensive
7. No opinion

See red box at the bottom of the page for the correct way to vote.

Here is how you *should* have voted:

1. 42%
2. 4%
3. 34%
4. 11%
5. 1%
6. 0%
7. 7%

[Source: http://www.topdatingtips.com/dating-statistics.htm]

that when the time is right things, will happen as they should whether he took her to the best steak house in town or for a java during their lunch break.

Being a gentleman also means doing simple acts of consideration and chivalry for your date and other women you encounter. If you do things like get doors, help her put on her coat, and pull out chairs, you could run into the occasional feminist who wants to "do it herself," but for the most part, women will love it. And think about it like this: wouldn't you like to find out sooner rather than later if she doesn't really want a real man but a real pansy? By the way, don't just open the door for hot girls or you'll look like a gigolo that treats some women like women and others like they're invisible. The one you like is watching to see if you're just posing or if you treat all women well.

INSTANT MESSAGE
from haze@marriable.com

See *How to Spot a Gigolo*, **page 67**.

As a gentleman you should also call her after the date to tell her you had a great time. But don't call her too soon or you'll seem desperate. Do it within two or three days. This also might be a good time to ask her out on the next date. Women love to hear from you after the date to recap and talk about how great things went. When you call you help her to know that you like her without appearing too desperate. Needless to say, don't talk about how desperate you

Continued on page 127

The Gentleman of Her Dreams

Men are always asking what women want. So now we're telling you. When it comes to dating, start with the basics. Respect your date. Think about what she likes—romance, to be sought after, to be considered beautiful, to be cared for—and apply those concepts to your interactions with her.

A gentleman:

never asks her out for a date less than three days before said date

always picks her up at the front door for the date

isn't late picking her up

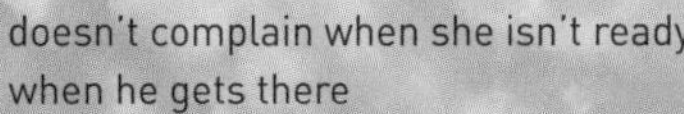
doesn't complain when she isn't ready when he gets there

has a plan for the evening and is prepared for changes in weather and/or activity

never asks her to pay for the date

doesn't check out other women when he's with her

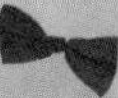
doesn't stare at her assorted body parts

always calls after the date to tell her he had a good time

doesn't apologize for being a man

are to see her again or how you can't live without her. Be cool, be kind, and listen, always listen.

Turning from Desperate to *Marriable*

The crux of this matter is that if you embrace being a real man, you will look a lot less like a desperate man and a lot more *Marriable*. If you've messed up in the past and played the fool by missing out on some of the more manly stuff about dating, then just shut up and fix it. Don't mope about the past; get on with the future. You can take the desperate out of your dating life and become the most *Marriable* guy in town if you are just willing to step up to the plate, risk yourself, and be a man. Remember, the best hitters in baseball strive to achieve the unbelievable level of getting a hit four out of ten times at the plate. Consider the advice in this book a form of legal performance-enhancing advice, only without the bloating.*

** In rare cases some bloating may occur if this book is consumed too rapidly and the mind does not have time to absorb it all.*

How to Compliment

Men and women want to be complimented in different ways. Don't compliment the way you want to be complimented, because it won't mean as much to the opposite sex. The basic thing you need to know is that **women like to be complimented on who they are.** Their beauty, their brains, their talents, things about them as a person. On the other hand, **men would rather be complimented on what they did** than on who they are.

Here is a chart to help clear things up:

Compliments for Men

- That was such a great idea.
- I never would have thought of that.
- Your shirt is really nice.
- I'm having a great time.
- I had so much fun tonight.
- I had a great time talking with you yesterday.
- That movie was great.

Compliments for Women

- You are so smart.
- I love how creative you are.
- You look amazing in that dress.
- You're so amazing.
- You are so much fun to be with.
- You are so great to talk to.
- You always pick the best movies.

Do we really need to explain the connection?

Women, Shut Up and Be Mysterious

> When men attempt bold gestures, generally it's considered romantic. When women do it, it's often considered desperate or psycho.
>
> Sarah Jessica Parker as Carrie
> from *Sex in the City*

> A foolish man tells a woman to stop talking, but a wise man tells her that her mouth is extremely beautiful when her lips are closed.
>
> Anonymous

Men love a challenge.

Let's say that again, all together: *Men love a challenge*. Any halfway objective observer can't help but notice that everything in Man World is either win or lose. And we do mean *everything*—from throwing away a wad of paper to comparing body parts, it's all a matter of competition. It's the fun in life for a guy, and that fun is centered around the hope that eventually he'll win more than he'll lose. Male bonding revolves around competition while female bonding revolves around communication. Men love the fight, the battle, the sweat, the chase. Maybe it harkens back to the days of the caveman clubbing Dino on the head for food. Hunt. Chase. Conquer. Eat. Live. Rinse. Repeat. But maybe there's more to it than even that. Maybe it's part of their DNA, the way they are wired to be unique and different from women and *for* women.

That's not to say that women don't want a challenge. They do. But the female challenge usually manifests itself somewhat differently, and here is where we begin to define that very challenge. A woman doesn't want a first date with a man who is already in the palm of her hand. Just like men, she likes the intrigue, the mystery, the challenge, the unread chapter. Not knowing if he is going to like her or not adds to her excitement.

But for the purposes of this chapter, we are going to concentrate on the challenge from the perspective of the man. Think of it like this: your challenge, ladies, is to learn how to become a challenge to him. Knowing how intriguing the suspense of the challenge is to you and understanding a bit of the male psyche, we will attempt to explain the best ways of becoming as *Marriable* as possible by becoming a woman of mystery.

Men are intrigued with women in general because there is something about women that they just don't get. You are mysterious—that is, until you open your mouth and attempt to wash away that mystery with the scouring pad of your tongue.

We've talked to many women in the course of writing this book and heard time and again about men who seemed very into them, even spent hours on the phone with them, but who suddenly and for no apparent reason quit calling. A lot of women bemoan the fact that he just doesn't seem that interested anymore. They can't understand where the excitement was lost and why he backed off. When we get a chance to watch these women in action on a date or with a group of men, we can see what might have happened. Though these women might understand that men love a challenge, they forget all about what a challenge is once the dating starts. They settle into the comfort of talking and sharing feelings and reveling in the excitement, and they completely forget about the intrigue and mystery that men so long for. And before you know it, any mystery that might have been there for the man is washed away with TMI—too much information. What women need to learn to tell themselves is "Shut up! He doesn't want to or need to hear everything that you want to or think you need to tell him."

Giving a man too much information is an act of selfishness. Most of the time the reason behind so much gabbing is that it feels good. That's not a reason to do something, especially in relationships. The successful and *Marriable* person understands that a relationship is more about giving the other person what they want than getting what we need—that is the true essence of unconditional love. When we make the relationship, especially early on, all about what we can get out of it, we lose. So the smart woman considers her audience and his desires, his needs, his genetic makeup, and determines that he's not female, and therefore, he does not bond by hearing me talk but by slowly discovering a little about me at a time. This is the true art of being a woman of mystery: understanding that giving yourself away as fast

Hayley,

The reason we divulge so much is because it makes us feel good. I feel like all these feelings inside me are just bursting to get out and be heard by someone. And a guy who is interested in me is like a captive audience. I want to tell him everything. Besides, it makes me feel more connected to him.

Michael,

I have to give you props, though. You controlled the feminine floodgates of information quite well . . . at least while we were dating! I remember telling you on more than one occasion that it was okay for you to call me, but it took awhile for you to do so, and I must say, it added to the mystery and fun of the chase. I wanted to chase you more. Once our relationship started rolling, I almost had to order you to call me.

Hayley,

And you thought you were in control. Talk about a win-win. You truly chased me till I caught you!

as possible makes the relationship boring for the man who loves a challenge. It's like playing a game of peek-a-boo with him when he really wants an almost impossible game of hide-and-seek. Boredom sets in easily in the relationship where too much is told too soon.

How Women Mess Up

From how they gab with their mouths to what they give with their bodies, women mess up the mystery factor in a variety of ways. Let's look at the most common mess-ups.

They Talk Too Much

Women mess up when they talk too much. We've never once heard a man say, "I just wish she'd talk more." Generally that's a female complaint. But have you ever thought that maybe he doesn't talk enough because you don't let him get a word in edgewise, ladies? Relationships are give and take. If the talking is all one-sided, don't blame it on him. Just maybe you are hogging all the words.

You've Got Quotes X

We've never once heard a man say, "I just wish she'd talk more."

We like to refer to women who talk too much as "giving up their emotional virginity." That is, they give away every ounce of themselves emotionally, and the result is the same as giving themselves up sexually—they are exposed and vulnerable to so much pain and heartache if and when the relationship ends.

Perhaps you've had great luck emptying your heart out on your date. Maybe you think you really just want to be honest and somehow honesty involves telling him *everything*. But something tells us that's not the case. So why not give shutting up a try?

They Chase Him

Many women will say that letting the man lead is an antiquated idea, and to that we say *hooey*! (An antiquated response.) When women chase men, they leave an imbalance in the relationship. The male's natural instinct to chase, to hunt, to pursue is suddenly useless. Why go out and hunt a rabbit when the rabbit has come up and laid itself at your feet? When the woman takes over the chase, the man might feel flattered at first. He might brag to his friends about his masculine prowess, but in time he will begin to resent his predicament. Then things like, "She is smothering me," will come out of his mouth. And what he really means is "She's chasing me and I'm bored with it. I need a challenge."

They Plan Everything

After a woman has pursued her man and "caught him," she rarely suddenly rests and falls back into object of pursuit mode. No, she has set the tone and will soon begin to run most aspects of their dating relationship. The next step of control is planning everything. The woman in this predicament complains about how the man never plans anything or does anything nice for her without ever realizing it's because she is doing it all for him. What she has created is a lazy man.

He knows that she is the one in charge and that she will take care of everything, so he relaxes and she powers on, praying that one day he'll be more involved. But a man rarely dives into a job that's already filled so adeptly by you.

The problem all started when she decided to chase him. The one who sets the tone of the chase continues it with the running of the relationship. For many women this sounds dreamy. They yearn to be in control; they crave the attention and the power that comes with being the one in the driver's seat. But watch these relationships and you will begin to see a funny transition: as the woman takes on more and more of the man's role, the man will naturally begin to take on more and more of the woman's role. He will become more passive, more weak even, and begin to withdraw from the relationship because he doesn't "feel quite right." When this happens, more often than not the woman tends to dive in even stronger and try to fix things by taking even more control, and the spiral spins further and further out of control. Terms like *nag, henpecked,* and *smothered* all come from men who have a controlling woman determined to make the relationship in her own image.

A man wants to be handpicked, not henpecked.

They Pay

An essential part of the pursuit of something you desire is the sacrifice you must make to get it. We always appreciate the things we worked hard for more than the things that were given us on a silver platter. When it comes to dating, part of the pursuit is paying for things. A man expresses his desire to love and care for a woman by providing for her, and the way he does that in the early stages of the relationship is by paying for food, fun, and gifts. Paying represents the chase that is so essential to the male need for challenge. Ladies, if you are on a date with a man and he asks you to pay, he is either telling you this is nothing but a friendship or that he is too much of a eunuch to be a man.

Hayley,

In defense of many a so-called "eunuch," I must say that the feminist stance on male-female relationships has probably confused them. Many men have believed the propaganda that women want so much equality that they want to pay for everything, get their own doors, and generally be indistinguishable from men.

Michael,

What these guys need to understand is that what most women want is to be thought of as equally intelligent and capable but not equal as in apples to apples.

Hayley,

We know we are different, and we love those differences. We love being pampered and cared for, pursued and desired. Don't believe the lie of equality that suddenly we want all the same roles and responsibilities as men. Find out what women want—it's different from what you want—and figure out how to give that to your woman, and she will love you forever.

They Give in Sexually

If you give too much physically, the result is just like being too emotionally vulnerable too soon—you have opened yourself up to experience all kinds of hurt, danger, and regret if the relationship ends. Giving too much of yourself before you have his undying commitment (i.e., marriage) is like giving a loan to someone who never intends to pay you back. That's a bad investment of yourself. A lot of women mistakenly think that giving him what he wants sexually will keep him coming back for more. But just like talking too much takes away the mystery, giving yourself to him sexually wipes out any hint of mystery you might have had left. Again, it has to do with the challenge. What challenge does a man have if the very thing he is ultimately after, your sex, is given to him way before he has paid the price for it? It makes you expendable. Don't waste your ace in the hole by giving him what he covets before he has proven that he won't take it and run.

5 Ways to Shut Up and Be Mysterious

The mysterious woman is always the woman who stands out. She's the one men can't resist. So what's the key to mystery? How do you close your open book and learn to first expose just the table of contents and then slowly, chapter by chapter, the pieces of your life? It's as simple as this: Shut up. Stop talking. We know it seems like an impossible suggestion—talking is life! If you don't talk, how do you get to know him? Think about it like this. You want him to follow you, right, because you have something he wants? Then rather than just dropping everything at his feet and then running off hoping he will chase you, try this. Drop a small morsel in front of him and let him partake of it. Then move on and drop another little morsel and see if he doesn't follow. Instead of gorging him on your words, give him just a taste at a time and he might just follow you wherever you go. Here's *5 Ways to Shut Up and Be Mysterious*:

#1 Keep part of your life to yourself—This has nothing to do with lying; it has to do with caring—caring how much of you the guy can handle. Remember, you've had a lifetime to experience your life, so don't shove it all down his throat in one phone call. Give him time to digest. Have you heard the cliché "save the best for last"? Think about that. It's very exciting when you've been dating someone awhile and they tell you something about them that you never knew. It is intriguing; it makes you want more. Leave them wanting more—that's the motto to live by.

#2 Limit your phone calls—The phone call is an oft-misinterpreted thing. Women and men translate the phone call differently. To a woman, the longer the phone call, the more he loves her. Women can grade the relationship on how much they talk, so that the 15-minute phone call means "I can't tell if he likes me or not," and the marathon call means "We were made for each other!" This is a really common female characteristic. We grade our relationships based on communication. "So how's it going with John?" your friend asks, and you say, "Amazing! We talked 3 hours last night. He is definitely the one." You never tell your friend, "It's the perfect relationship. We talk 15 minutes every night; he's really into me." That's because communication is the subject that carries the highest grade-point value in the female school of dating. We covet it the most.

The man, however, looks at things through different lenses. You never hear a guy say to his buddy, "She's definitely the one because, boy, can she talk!" When he gets off the phone with his love, he doesn't call his best friend to give him a blow-by-blow of the conversation and revel in the communication.

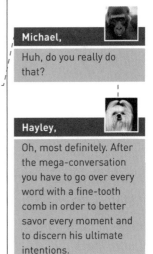

Michael,

Huh, do you really do that?

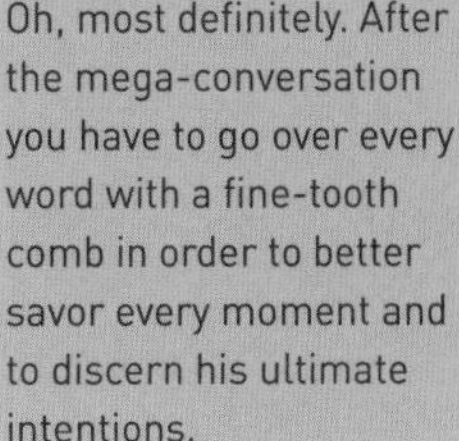
Hayley,

Oh, most definitely. After the mega-conversation you have to go over every word with a fine-tooth comb in order to better savor every moment and to discern his ultimate intentions.

Women and men see talking differently. To see this in the wild, all you need to do is observe how much time men spend on the phone chatting with their friends versus how much time women spend doing the same. Men bond differently, and talking is just not what gets them hot or gets them interested.

So knowing this about the male species gives women a lot of ammo. If he isn't turned on to you by talking, then how about by not getting enough? Wouldn't you rather overhear him say, "Man, I just can't seem to get enough of her," than "That girl can sure talk"? So the rule of thumb in managing your communication with the guy you want to land is this: keep the phone calls short. Leave him wanting more. The best idea is to set a timer to 15 minutes. This might seem inhumane to the female reader, but guys are reading this and thinking, *Phew!* You can talk about all you need to talk about in 15 minutes, and if you can't, then you'll definitely be leaving him wanting more. At the end of 15 minutes when you say, "Gee, I've had a great time talking to you, but I gotta go," he'll flip. His mind will start to wonder, *What does she have to do? Why did she hang up?* And the mystery is on. Of course, after you've started to date officially, you can allow the conversation to go longer, but try not to let them drag on. Remember, always leave him wanting more.

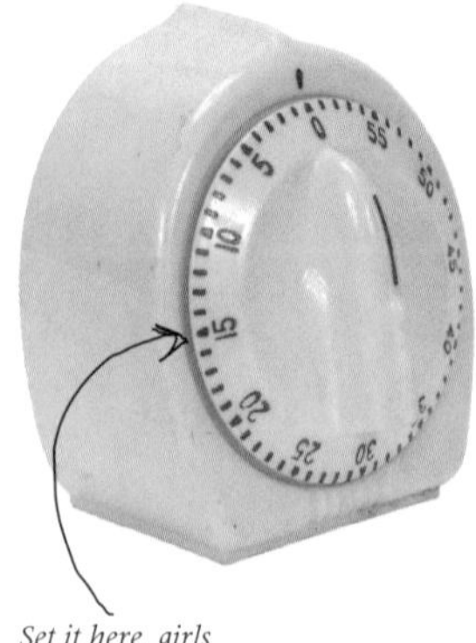

Set it here, girls.

Honesty note: If you feel funny saying you have to go when you don't, then make plans for yourself. Plan to wash your hair in 15 minutes. Plan on going for a walk, starting dinner, whatever it might be. A woman who gives of herself sparingly in the beginning of a relationship is a woman of mystery.

#3 No last-minute date—It's really hard to say no to a date, any date, but you have to be strategic in becoming a woman of mystery. If he calls for a Saturday night date on Friday, then he's at the end of his list or just a really lousy planner, or maybe he just doesn't know the days of the week yet. Either way, he needs to understand that you are not a last-minute date. If he wants to go out with you, he needs to plan, he needs to prep, he needs to make reservations. You're not McDonald's; you're the finest restaurant in town that everyone is dying to get reservations for. This is all part of giving the man what he loves, the chase. Something that is easy to get is never as coveted as something that is hard to get. So as hard as it is to say, "Sorry, I already have plans, but maybe next week," you have to say it. When you do, you up your value; you go from booty call to woman of mystery in 15 seconds. So the rule of thumb here is, if he wants to go out with you this weekend, he has to call you before Thursday or you're busy. Again, for those of you fearful of "lying," think about it like this: no matter what the situation, you *will* be doing something this weekend. Whether it's renting movies and eating ice cream or redecorating your room, you *will* be doing *something*, so you aren't lying to him. And if a completely uncouth guy actually *asks* what you are doing, play the mystery card and say, "Wow, that's none of your business." Because it really isn't. Don't think you have to be an open book to be an honest person. You don't.

#4 Don't whine—As part of their love of communication, women have a tendency to describe everything they are feeling, even if it's bad. This is called whining, and it's ugly. The male psyche is such that when you whine, he hears, "You aren't doing things right." His success at caring for you is obliterated when you whine about things; it makes him feel like he is to blame for your discomfort. And chances are, he isn't. But even if

Whiners (and drunks) are not mysterious.

he is, give the guy a break. Contrary to how you might see yourself, you are not a princess who needs things to be perfect in order to survive. Be tough. Don't expect the world to cater to your every need and whim, and you will become a real woman of mystery. Men love women who have fun, not women who complain about not having fun. So lighten up.

#5 Don't talk about other women—Gossip, you have to admit, can be fun. Even though we know it's bad, it's still something we often can't resist. It's part of female bonding. But when it comes to men, lay off. They really don't like it. What they hear when you talk bad about another woman is your insecurity. You look really cheap and insecure, which are very unattractive traits in a woman. Remember, men don't order their lives around talking, communicating, and knowing everything about everyone. Just the facts, ma'am, that's all they need. Gossip doesn't score you any points with men, so lay off when he's within earshot.

Turning Desperate into *Marriable*

Ladies, when you practice these ways to shut up and be mysterious, two things happen. First, you protect the mystery, which causes the guy to want to find out more by pursuing you more. Second, the mystery ups your social value. When you have something else to do besides sit on the phone and chat all night, you become a woman whose time is valuable, or at least appears to be. When you can't go out at the last minute, a guy will try to figure out how to get on your calendar. And you will become much more *Marriable*.

Hopefully you see now that when we say *shut up and be mysterious,* we have nothing but love in store for you. We want you to be confident. We want you to be the powerful woman you were made to be. We want you to be in control of your own *Marriability*.

Is it time to pick on the men yet?!

EXTRA! EXTRA!
I finished in last place!

Nice Guys Really Do Finish Last

"Nice guys finish last, but we get to sleep in."

Evan Davis, author

Throughout history a well-documented gripe has been that *nice guys finish last.* In our observation of reality TV dating shows (an excellent way to understand the sicker side of dating), we have found that the first guys "voted off" are "nice guys." For centuries "nice guys" have been saying, "I just need to treat her like crap and maybe then she'll like me." While we completely understand why a man might resort to this throwing-in-of-the-towel, it is not an entirely correct behavior modification. So before we make a bad situation worse, let's investigate the following hypothesis: *she doesn't dislike you because you're nice, she dislikes you because you're too transparent.*

The problem with the nice guy isn't that he's too nice; it's that he's too fast in giving up his emotions and his heart. For men to have emotions is okay and even normal, but to readily *express* them is a more feminine trait. Whether this comes from social programming or divine design, it is now the status quo. Because of this, women tend to set the emotional tone and rate of emotional disclosure in relationships. If the man is more emotional than the woman, she feels off balance. It seems

I Wanted to Say "I Love You"

by Hayley

I remember the point when Michael and I were dating when I decided for sure that I was "desperately" in love with him. The words "I love you" had not yet been spoken, but I longed to say them. Yet I knew I wanted him to be the first to say them. He was sublime in his observation of my giddiness and gushiness. He seemed to know exactly at what point I was ready to confess my love, and then and only then did he, after making me suffer for several hours, say "I love you." It was divine. The dance was pure romance. I was there emotionally well before he confessed that he was too.

like overkill because she isn't that emotional yet. When the nice guy takes over the emotional speed control, he can seem rather girly.

INSTANT MESSAGE
from bobismydog@marriable.com

See *Study Confirms That Showing Emotions Is a Female Characteristic*, **page 150**.

In contrast, the "bad boy" appears attractive to the woman because he doesn't go too fast emotionally, he isn't as transparent, and thus he is more manly in her eyes. He never initiates the "define the relationship" conversation early on in the relationship (or ever, probably) because he's not looking for commitment. And besides, it's painfully obvious that she digs him and wants him to commit, because he's allowed her to fall madly, gushingly in love with him by not drowning her in sentiment. Note that we are not saying that the bad boy is a good thing, only that early on in the relationship he seems to understand what a woman needs. However, as the relationship progresses, the bad boy has his own set of "issues" to deal with. What we will attempt to explore here is how to blend the good characteristics of the bad boy with the good characteristics of the nice guy to make a *Marriable* man. The key is to be more of a bad boy early on and a nice guy as the relationship progresses and the female is ready for more emotion from the male.

One event that's never easy is the "three little words" scenario. In this scenario the male senses the female's level of involvement with him and keeps pace with her. For example, when he is certain that she is dying to say "I love you," then and only then does he first say "I love you" so that he may take the lead at the appropriate time. If he were to say "I love you" too soon, before she was ready, then he would risk appearing like the "nice guy," too emotionally involved too soon. As she moves the emotional meter further and further along the continuum, the conscientious male monitors her levels and performs the delicate dance that allows him to always be leading her emotionally yet only to the extent that she is already there. The big double standard for guys to accept is this:

Michael,

Now that I think about it, the nice guys probably need to read *Shut Up and Be Mysterious* just as much as the women. That sure would've helped me back in my "nice guy" days.

Hayley,

Yeah, anybody who gives too much emotional information too soon, regardless of gender, needs to shut up and be mysterious!

Hayley,

I once said "I love you" to a guy and his reply was "Thank you." What was that? It would have been better for him to say absolutely nothing!

Michael,

Where does he live? I'll beat him up! Wait, that doesn't make sense. Beat him up because he doesn't love you? Never mind.

Michael,

You know, I think guys would understand this with a sports analogy. The bad boy has the game plan for the first half of the game, but he can't make adjustments at halftime to close things out. The nice guy's scouting report is all wrong; he's blown out by halftime and was never in the game.

Hayley,

Huh?

Michael,

Trust me, *guys* get it.

guy says "I love you" before girl is ready = turnoff

girl says "I love you" before guy is ready = still in the game

Guys, you can rescue your almost-loved-one with this response: NEVER say it back if she's the first one to say it. If you think you're never going to feel it, you need to use this opportunity to let her know. But if you do love her, somewhere along the line you missed the signs of her love. You'll need to recreate the event so you can say it "first," showing her you are able to read and lead her emotionally. Things will be awkward, but be patient. Cover your tracks with "We've got something special here, let's keep it going," and regroup.

She'll most likely be crushed or at the very least embarrassed with your nonresponse, but she'll never have to wonder if you just said it because she said it. Plan a recovery date and unleash the three words of mass destruction.

You need to understand the important fact that the "bad" in the "bad boy" isn't what really ultimately attracts the female; the *male* in the bad boy is what attracts her. The bad boy lacks overtly female characteristics, so early on he is an easier place for the female psyche to find what she craves in a man—maleness. The nice guy's maleness might be hidden behind his "feminine side" and therefore be harder for the female to spot. With a few adjustments to communication and presentation, however, the nice guy can learn to release the varying aspects of his personality at appropriate times, thus intriguing the female more adeptly.

The Initial Attraction of the Bad Boy

The bad boy that girls squirm over typically seems to have a well-defined personality. He has a style all his own. He has a suave confidence that might almost look like arrogance to some, but at least he knows who he is and what he wants. He's a man's man. Firm, silent, confident. He doesn't smile a lot like a schoolgirl. He doesn't get overly excited or giddy. He doesn't have a bunch of girlfriends who consider him just one of the girls. He has the typically male characteristics that draw the attention of the female. When he picks her up for a date, he isn't standing at attention like a love-struck schoolboy; he is calm and casual, in control. If he offers flowers, they look almost like an afterthought, not a bouquet he spent hours searching for. His understated actions make the female think perhaps he's had so much experience dating that it isn't anything new . . . and that must mean a lot of girls like him . . . and therefore he must be quite a catch. Follow the female logic?

You know, it only took me three decades or so to learn that logic, and I have *four* sisters.

Girls yearn for the bad boy because he seems to know more than he's letting on. He doesn't gush over her. He clearly likes her, but he's holding something back, and that's intriguing. He isn't afraid to ask her out or to take her hand or to lead the way. In her estimation he is a real man, and what's most important is that he makes her feel like a real woman. Why? Because he has no female characteristics that compete with her own. Instead, he seems to need her to bring the female traits to the relationship. It's a perfect union, each filling in where the other is lacking.

Continued on page 151

STUDY #:YduIcr-i

Study Confirms That Showing Emotions Is a Female Characteristic

NASHVILLE, Tenn. – Men and women experience the same level of sadness while watching tearjerkers like *Titanic*—but women are more likely to reach for a box of tissues. That is the conclusion of Vanderbilt University psychologist Ann Kring, whose findings on sex differences in emotion have appeared in the American Psychological Association's *Journal of Personality and Social Psychology*.

"It is incorrect to make a blanket statement that women are more emotional than men," she says. "It is correct to say that women show their emotions more than men."

Kring conducted two studies—one to determine whether women are "more emotional" or just "more expressive" and the other to explore whether gender roles account for expressive differences between women and men. In both studies, women were found to be more facially expressive of both positive and negative emotions.

In both studies, university students were brought individually into a laboratory setting and told that they were participating in a study of the psychology of movies and what aspect of a movie draws people into the plot. To prevent the subjects from modifying their behavior, nothing about emotions was mentioned. Subjects were then secretly videotaped. In addition, electrodes were attached to their hands to monitor palm-sweating, a measure of emotion.

"We decided to see if maybe sex isn't the important variable in emotional expressiveness since there are such predominant stereotypes about sex and emotion," says Kring. "Maybe it's not sex that contributes to these emotion differences, but something called gender role."

Feminine gender roles traditionally include such attributes as being nurturing, affectionate, warm, and caring, while masculine characteristics are generally the opposite: being aggressive, powerful, and assertive.

Significantly, both male and female participants endorsing a high number of characteristics traditionally associated with both masculinity and femininity were more facially expressive. They also reported having a more expressive disposition than participants reporting only a high number of either masculine or feminine characteristics.[8]

Why Nice Guys Finish Last on a Date

Now let's have a look at the "nice guy." This is the guy who is all about the girl. He listens intently, he responds appropriately, he talks of his heart and his feelings just as he's been told that girls like. He is transparent and giving of his emotions and his thoughts. He wants to create a bond with the girl that is similar to one she might have with her best friend. He caters to her every need; he even anticipates them. And these things aren't bad in themselves, but when it begins to appear that he lives for the attention of the female, she starts to wonder. "So early in the relationship and he already seems to think I hung the moon. He obviously doesn't know me," she thinks to herself. "Am I his last and only option?" His premature and inaccurate estimate of her perfection leaves her suspicious. And when he makes it very clear early on that he adores her, even loves her, the jig is up. The girl can no longer handle the overly emotional and emotive male who seems to be responding like *she* longs to respond in a healthy relationship. Essentially he takes her role on himself and rides it like a weary horse. This leaves the girl feeling anything but feminine.

Bad Boy Bonus—Later on, if the bad boy were to grow with his mate emotionally, he might find a healthier relationship. Many women beg for their men to be more emotional. At that point, emotions are a good thing and the bad boy needs to learn to give a little.

Is it easier for the bad boy to add enough niceness to become *Marriable* or for a nice guy to add the bad boy characteristics? The answer is that it doesn't matter. Both should move toward a position of balance, understanding the needs of the female and his role as a male.

UPGRADE NICEGUY 1.3

Upgrade NOW to MARRIABLEGUY 2.0 Includes "virtual badboy" code for increased compatibility.

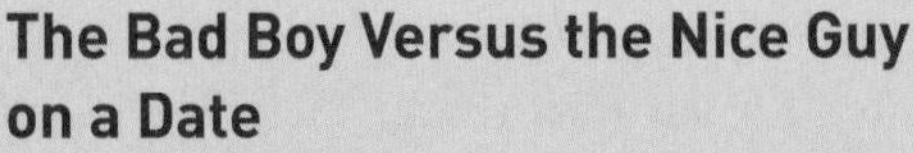

The Bad Boy Versus the Nice Guy on a Date

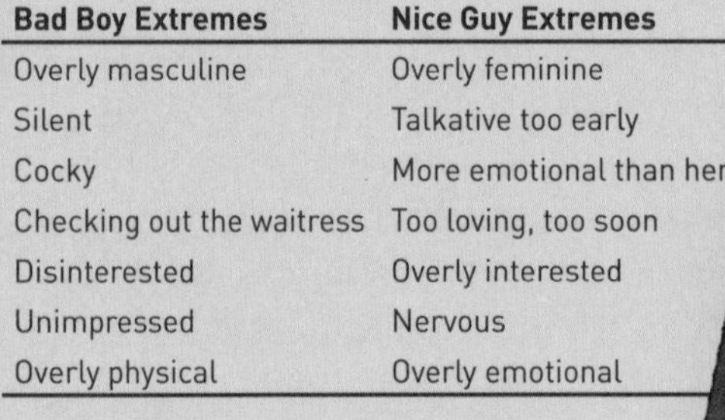

Bad Boy Extremes	Nice Guy Extremes
Overly masculine	Overly feminine
Silent	Talkative too early
Cocky	More emotional than her
Checking out the waitress	Too loving, too soon
Disinterested	Overly interested
Unimpressed	Nervous
Overly physical	Overly emotional

Note: What bad boys (and girls) have learned is that the bad boy extremes win out over the nice guy extremes every time. While the nice guy extremes are less harmful, most women would rather have the bad boy. Any of you ladies who might have been reading this and saying, "Oh, I'd take the nice guy over the bad boy any day," consider this: Are you looking for a man or a lap dog? Seriously, if you want a guy who is at your beck and call, aren't you essentially looking for a loyal follower? One who will cater to all your needs? In this kind of position, the female is bound to lead an unbalanced relationship that will turn a nice guy into a quietly angry guy. Ahh, bliss.

Steps toward Never Hearing Again, "You're a Nice Guy, But . . ."

If you, the male of the relationship, have ever said something like, "How come you act more like a man than a girl?" then you've just diagnosed yourself as the nice guy. So what do you do now? How do you make sure that your next dating adventure doesn't end in friendship alone? Here are some steps to help you become less of a nice guy and more a guy she wants:

1. **Don't tell her you love her too early on.** Make sure she is dying to hear you say it before you ever do.
2. **Don't get too far ahead of her emotionally.** Women love a guy who knows how to lead. Guys should define the relationship. When the time comes, say "I love you" first, and keep the relationship on track, but part of this is knowing your timing. Get too far ahead of her emotionally and you lose.
3. **Don't talk more than she does.** Sure, girls love a guy who talks with her, but she also likes to be heard, so don't try to compete with her in the area of talking. Always lag a bit behind to keep her guessing.
4. **Have a life.** Guys who suddenly make the girl their entire life are boring. Girls want to see you with your friends, playing sports, working on cars, whatever—just have a life so she doesn't feel like she has to support you emotionally. That's your job for her, not hers for you, early on in the dating relationship. (Note: as the relationship progresses toward and into marriage, the relationship grows and matures, and all of these things change. But you're making a mistake if you take the relationship there too quickly. That only makes you just another nice guy. We are talking about getting you *Marriable*, and this puts you in a better position.)

Attention men! Women want to feel feminine, and the quickest way to help them feel feminine is to be masculine.

In November 1937, Al Capp, cartoonist and creator of the famous Li'l Abner comic strip, created a character known as Sadie Hawkins. Li'l Abner ran in the magazine The National Review from the mid-1930s until the mid-1950s and depicted a backwoods American town known as Dogpatch, USA.

According to the story, Sadie Hawkins was the ugly daughter of the richest and most powerful man in town. In spite of her family's wealth, Sadie was avoided by all the men in town. And her father feared that because of this, she would end up with the worst fate of all—becoming an old maid.

So he devised a plan to help her catch a man. He lined up all the eligible men and shot his gun. When the gun was fired, they ran for their lives and their singleness, because right behind them were all the unmarried women in town, chasing after them to catch the men who would become their husbands.

Sadie seemed to be as fast as she was ugly and quickly caught her a man. The girls who weren't so lucky liked the idea so much that they made it an annual event where they could attempt to capture the man of their dreams.

Capp came up with the idea of a Sadie Hawkins Day dance, for which the girls would take the initiative and ask out the guys. The idea caught on like wildfire in schools across America and still continues today.

Turning Desperate into *Marriable*

In review, nice guys are desperate to share too much too soon, and bad boys are desperate to bury their softer side as flawed weakness. Meanwhile, back on the Estrogen Ranch, girls who date bad boys are desperate to believe they can change them, and girls who date nice guys are soon freaked out when the niceys share too much too soon. Reversing these habits and patterns in your dating life will not only increase your *Marriability* but also help you choose more *Marriable* people to date.

Remember, nice guys finish last and bad boys aren't far behind.

I have a problem with intimacy,
hence the firewall.

Online Dating: Not Just for the Desperate Anymore

40 million people date online per day.

VH1, "The Wild World of Online Dating," 2003

The Internet is an amazing thing. It can lead people to love, it can lead people astray, and if used properly, it could be the answer to your dating dilemma. But the Internet doesn't save us from ourselves. We still have to work on our own *Marriability*, guard our hearts, and do the right research, or we'll end up just as desperate in cyberspace as we are in public space. Who knows? Online dating might just be the answer to your dating dreams, like it was for us. But before you set sail on the cyber-sea of love, make sure you know how to manage the wind in your sails.

The Benefits of Online Dating

Choices, Choices, Choices (And Did We Mention Choices?)

Have you ever complained, "I just don't know where to meet people" or "All the good ones are taken." While that might have been true in your little hamlet before the days of Internet dating, it most definitely isn't true anymore. Your workplace or church is a small, finite pool of potentials, and once you've discovered that the one for you isn't where you spend your time, then maybe it's time to look in a bigger pool.

The world has become a much smaller place. People are now dating people in other cities, other states, and even other countries. When we met online, we lived over 2,000 miles apart, but that didn't hinder us. In fact, it gave us a better opportunity to get to know one another without all the sexual tension that can taint the waters when dating someone face-to-face. All we could do for months in between visits was talk, and that taught us a lot about each other. Dating online is one of the best things we've ever done. So don't be afraid to try it, and you'll definitely find many more choices available to you than your hometown can provide.

Someday, my prince will log on.

First Contact

The first impulse you may have when logging on to this newfound cyber mate-market is to run around like a kid in a candy store, emailing every hottie in sight. But slow down, player! Let's get some online etiquette down first. For the ladies, the thing you must remember is that guys are the same in cyberspace as they are in real life. Real men want to make the first move. But before you start feeling powerless to attract the hordes of men online, most quality dating sites have subtle "first contact" tools that tell guys who has viewed their profile and when. One visit to a guy's profile, and then you can watch to see if he visits yours. Add him to your "favorites" list and (on the better dating sites) he can tell. If after a few repeated visits he doesn't get the hint, he's probably not interested. Don't worry, there's plenty more where he came from.

Also, don't use the excuse that "he probably just hasn't logged on for a while, so I'd better email him." Technology has taken care of that as well; you can see how long it's been since his last log-on! It's just like seeing the same attractive stranger in your favorite coffee shop every day. After a while, you'll notice if they notice you.

Gentlemen, sometimes a first contact email is too much of an unexpected shock to a woman's system without some more subtle cyber-brushes first. Use some of the tips above, and take advantage of some of the other pre-email flirting tools available on these sites. Usually every advanced site has a "flirt," "smile," or "wave" button that shoots a short predetermined message to the object of your flat-panel desire. Consider these cyber–socially acceptable pickup lines, ones that won't get you cyber-slapped. These are a safer intro than pouring out your dreams in the first email or simply forwarding the same form letter to 600 women per second.

Second Contact or No Contact

So you've either made first contact or had first contact made with you—now what? If you are

Continued on page 162

Decoding Online Profile of the Desperate (girls)

princess53 –
Age: 33
Gender: Female
A Little About Me: I love getting to know people. I'm looking for someone just to hang out with and have fun with, no strings attached. If you are looking for a distraction then send me a note. I really just want to find friends here and hope you are looking for the same thing. I'm fun to be with and spend a lot of time on the go. Need someone who is active. I love the outdoors, but I also love getting dressed up and going out on the town. I'm the life of the party and never at a loss for words.
Marital Status: Single
Height: 5'10"
Eyes: Green
Hair: Blonde
Sense of Humor: Life of the party, comic relief
Career: Marketing
Personality: Outgoing, assertive, loveable
Education: College grad
Interests: skeet shooting, sky diving, skiing, adventure

Desperate decoded –

diva53 –
Age: really 38 but don't want old men picking up on me
Gender: Female
A Little About Me: Too many guys are after me so I'm telling everyone I just want to be friends. That way when I reject you, you won't be too hurt. If only one of you would step up and be a man and quit acting like a love-struck school girl I might actually date you. My life is non-stop, and forget about going Dutch, be prepared to open your wallet to keep up. I talk a lot, so be ready to do a lot of listening.
Marital Status: Engaged 3 times
Height: 5'10"
Eyes: Green contact lenses
Hair: Blonde (again, every four weeks)
Sense of Humor: always the center of attention . . . or at least I better be
Career: Marketing
Personality: Domineering, aggressive, bossy
Education: College grad
Interests: Any expensive date

Decoding Online Profile of the Desperate (guys)

Bigdaddylove223 –
Age: 28
Gender: Male
A Little About Me: I'm old school. I love the eighties. I want a woman who wants the same things as I do. Not too high maintenance, but likes to be playful. I'm still a boy at heart. I live in a funky apartment with my dog. He's a great animal, I'm sure you will love him. I'm not a real big outdoorsman, so if you like staying at home and just relaxing, I'm your man.
Marital Status: Single
Height: 6'0"
Eyes: Brown
Hair: Brown
Ethnicity: Caucasian
Sense of Humor: Uh, what's that?
Career: Technology entrepreneur
Personality: Analytical, easygoing, contemplative
Education: College
Interests: Anything cutting edge

Desperate decoded –

Biglazylove223 –
Age: 28
Gender: Male
A Little About Me: I can't let go of the past. I still live at home in an apartment over my mom's garage. I don't want a woman who demands too much of me because I'm lazy. You have to love animals if you want to love me because I'm not kicking him out of bed at night. All I like to do is lock myself in my room and play video games. It's my life. I've created an entire Sims world for myself that I really love. If you want to be my Sims partner then send me a note.
Marital Status: Single
Height: 5'9"
Eyes: Brown
Hair: Brown
Ethnicity: Caucasian
Sense of Humor: I don't get it
Career: Buy and sell video games on eBay for a profit.
Personality: Boring, live in a fantasy world
Education: College for 2 weeks, gave up because I couldn't get out of bed
Interests: Anything teenage guys do.

Hayley,

I was surprised by how many guys got mad at me for not responding to their electronic advances. They didn't seem to think I should form my own opinions of them. I should just take their word for it that they were the one for me. And if for some reason I rejected them, it was because I was stuck up, stupid, or a "witch." You have to get a tough skin, because you get first contact in cyberspace much more often than you ever got it in real life.

Michael,

My biggest problem was getting over the feeling that I was obligated to email everybody back and tell them nicely why I wasn't interested. Yeah, nothing feels better than having to write a rejection letter every day when you open your email. That's not what cyberspace is all about. You don't say hi every time you see a friend log on to IM. Remember, it's not like you're ever going to see these people. That's not a license to be rude or brutal, but ignoring their advances isn't a crime.

reading what seems to be a form letter, if the first email is way too personal way to soon, or if you're just not interested, hit delete. This person doesn't know what they're doing, and you've got a mate to find. Imagine if you had to explain to everyone who flirted with you why you didn't flirt back. You'd get nothing done in the world. You don't have to explain. If someone doesn't get the hint, keeps emailing you, and is belligerent in nagging you to respond, quality sites will have a blocking feature so you can type in the person's user name and keep them from communicating with you or seeing when you are online anymore. It's a great invention for dealing with cyber-jerks.

Save Time

When you start to date online, you soon find out that you can sift through a lot of "potentials" much quicker online than you can face-to-face. You can instantly delete all the form letter emails and all the way too personal emails with the click of a button. When you find someone who looks interesting and start to talk to them, you can find out a lot about them without ever having to get emotionally involved. You know those dates you go on where by the end of the night you are most definitely sure the person isn't the one for you but the other person for some reason doesn't feel the same way? Think about how much easier it is to move on online than face-to-face. All it takes is a note saying good-bye. You don't have to worry about them continuing to call, or coming by your house, or bothering your friends. Online dating is a clean way to maintain your boundaries in dating and avoiding wasting time on people you already know (or are soon to find out) aren't for you.

A 15-minute online conversation can tell you all you need to know. And guys, you get a special bonus because you save yourself the cost of a date as well as the time. Online dating allows you to sift through hundreds if not thousands of people in a short time and potentially get to the really good ones much quicker than in traditional dating.

Safety

In the old days, women worried about meeting strangers and giving out their phone numbers. They did it all the time, but it always brought a chance of danger. If all your friends have exhausted the blind-dating list and you've already met all the eligible ones at church, online dating is the next safest thing. Now you can spend time getting to know someone without divulging your identity or vital statistics like home address, and that brings much less chance of violence. Of course, you still have to be careful once you find someone you'd like to know more about, but if you know all the ins and outs of online dating, you can secure your safety just as well as you can on a blind date.

Here are some things you should consider before you dive into the World Wide Web of dating.

Stay Anonymous Early On

The best thing about online dating from a safety perspective is your ability to remain anonymous until you are ready to take a relationship further. This allows you to chat and to get to know people well before you meet them. But staying anonymous isn't always easy.

Hayley,

I thought I was such a smart girl when I first signed on to a dating site. I got myself a Yahoo email address that wasn't connected to my work so no one would know who I was. I was being so anonymous, or so I thought. But after I had emailed Michael from that account, he wrote me back and said, "You'd better change the 'name' field on your email profile, because next to your emails it says 'Hayley Morgan.'" Dang! That small fact had eluded me. I gave away my identity immediately—luckily, it was only to my future husband, but if it had been a crazy nut (other than Michael) I could have been in some trouble. So protect your anonymity. It's a great way to maintain your boundaries in online dating.

Here are some ways to hide who you are from your online dates and rejects:

Create an anonymous email address. Don't put your last name in the application for the email account, or it will show up when you email.

INSTANT MESSAGE from bobismydog@marriable.com

Visit www.marriable.com for a list of free email services.

Be careful not to use a signature line (name, address, phone, etc.) in your emails.

Never tell them your last name, where you work, or your home phone number.

When you get to the point where you're ready for a phone call, use caller ID block to call an online date. Women, don't give them your number till you really feel safe. Too many websites will give you an address to go with a phone number.

Guard Yourself

Don't fall too fast.

Don't divulge too much about yourself.

Don't create a nickname that will make you a target—hotsister, richman, or sexywoman probably aren't the best.

Do Some Detective Work

Don't believe everything you read.

Get more than one picture of the person—if they only have one picture, it could be of anybody, even a model from a picture frame. But it's pretty hard to fabricate two pictures of a sexy stranger.

Do research. If they've said what city they are in and what kind of work they do, see if you can't find out what company they work for. Google their names. Don't be a stalker in your research, but make sure the things they are telling you about themselves match public information you can get straight off the web.

Hayley,

I knew from Michael's profile what kind of job he had and what city he lived in, so I did a search of companies in his city that did the kind of work he did. It didn't take me long to figure out where he worked.

Michael,

The challenge is doing investigative work without being a stalker. In other words, you might be totally crafty and figure out where she works and what street she lives on by the second email. But for goodness' sake, don't tell her just to "show off" how ingenious you are! That is, unless your user name is stalkerdude911 . . .

Go Slow

Talk on the phone only after you've had some time to get to know each other and you've done your research. Talk on the site for enough time to notice any red flags like these:

Their answers change a lot—age, interests, profession, etc. That's a sure sign of a liar.

They try to guilt you into telling them your full name and/or phone number.

They won't answer any direct questions even after a fair amount of time has passed. What do they have to hide?

Be Cautious about Meeting Face-to-Face

When you're ready, arrange to meet in a public place and make sure someone you trust knows about it and has access to information on your date. Your date should never be upset when you put safety first.

Here are a few rules of thumb that will keep the mystery and help ensure your safety when meeting in person.

- The man should come to the woman's city.
- Don't tell your date the name of your hotel.
- Each of you should drive yourself to and from the date.
- Don't tell your date your address.
- Meet in a public place.
- Tell a friend where you are going.
- Travel note: If a guy flies a long distance to your city, that's a big expense, and some jerks will expect a physical payoff for their efforts. If a guy is making a long-distance trek to meet you for the first time, be direct in saying ahead of time "Are you sure about this? 'Cause for you this is going to be one expensive cup of coffee." That way he'll know up front that this is just like any other first date that you would have if you lived in the same city.

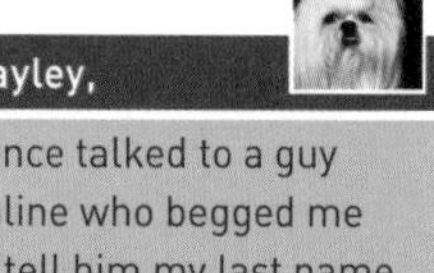

Hayley,

I once talked to a guy online who begged me to tell him my last name before we had even made plans to meet. I told him I couldn't because then he'd know who I was. He got really irate and said I was arrogant, as if I were some big star or something. I ended that "relationship" quickly. That was a definite red flag. Freak!

Michael,

I learned my lesson, though—I just created a new identity and emailed you again, Clarice.

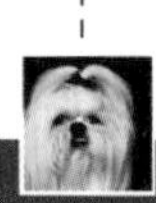

Hayley,

Aaaahhhhh! Please, no *Silence of the Lambs* imagery!

Long-Distance Dating

If you start a long-distance relationship, you might need to try some creative ways to bridge the dating distance:

- Spend a night IM-ing poetry to each other.
- Sign up for an online game like Wheel of Fortune or Trivial Pursuit and play it together.
- Watch the same TV show and talk about it on the phone while you watch.
- Read books on relationships and then talk about your thoughts later that night.

Creating the Best First Impression Profile

Don't flatter yourself. Be honest. Don't hype yourself up; people can see right through that. But don't be negative about yourself either. Who wants to be with a downer? Be honest, but hold back some information for when they contact you.

Don't lie. You may be really tempted to forget to mention your two kids or that you're out of work, but be careful not to lie, because once you start a relationship with someone, they will find out the truth eventually, and then you'll look like a complete idiot.

Include a picture. Lots of people say, "I want them to like me for *me*, not my looks." And to that

Hi. I'm 29, colorful, and loaded with potential.

Online dating profile.

This frog is a total liar. He's really 34.

Hayley,

When I was dating online, I just skipped right over any profile that didn't have a picture, because who wants to start a relationship with someone to whom you might turn out to have absolutely no attraction at all? And besides, you can't really trust a profile without a picture; the photo is just another step in divulging the real you, which allows the other person to trust you. Don't be afraid of how you look. Someone out there will think you are just adorable!

we say, *phooey*. We all judge people by how they look, especially someone we want to date.

More than one picture is good, if you have them. It lets everyone know that you didn't just upload a photo from a frame you bought. But don't overdo it either. Only use up to four photos.

Make sure they can see you. If you are scaling a mountain in the picture, they might see your interests, but they won't be able to see you. Make sure they can see your face in your photo.

Stay clothed. When guys show themselves shirtless, they just look trashy. When women do it, guys, check the web address on your browser—you probably stumbled onto a porn site. Sickos!

Don't include a photo of you with your ex or anyone else of the opposite sex. Everyone assumes it's someone you are dating or just broke up with, and that's creepy.

Don't overemphasize your sexiness. Glamour shots or posing in front of your Porsche only makes people laugh. Simplicity is best. Remember, the purpose of the photo is for others to see if you look like someone they might fall in love with.

Turning Desperate into *Marriable*

When we couldn't find love among our circle of friends, our coworkers, and our church families, we simply expanded our circle from the comfort of our own homes . . . to a 2,000-mile radius. And why not? In the age of email, Instant Messaging, free long-distance, and unlimited nights and weekends, the world is getting smaller. And when we "met" online all those miles away, what did we find? That we were born 26 days apart, 60 miles apart. That while a teenage Michael was busing tables on weekends at a local restaurant, teenage Hayley and her mom would come to Michael's "big city" to shop the mall and eat at the very same restaurant. Do you have a story like that waiting? Love may be only a click away.

Michael,

I chatted online for a while with a girl who seemed normal enough, but she wouldn't post a picture where I could see her head to toe. After much asking, she sent more pics, but in every one of them, she was behind a bunch of friends or peeking around a wall, and I thought *What's the deal?* Come to find out, she was self-conscious about her body. To me, that was a turnoff—not because of her weight but because she was hiding something that had nothing to do with her safety. Long story short, don't post pictures of how you looked five years ago at your sister's wedding. Be real.

INSTANT MESSAGE
from bobismydog@marriable.com

Log on to www.marriable.com for a ton of online dating reviews, tips, and more.

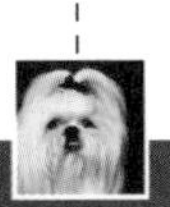

Hayley,

I can top that. I once got an email through a dating site from a *blind man* who told me, "My pastor said that you look like someone I would like." He was about 20 years older than me and definitely not my type. Telling him I wasn't interested was the hardest Internet rejection I ever had to give. Poor guy. How can a woman tell a blind man she isn't interested when his pastor tells him to email her? Ugh! But I did it. I wasn't about to lead the guy on.

He sure looks like a nice guy on the surface, but is he really *Marriable?*

Marriable vs. Divorceable

> When I meet a guy, the first question I ask myself is: is this the man I want my children to spend their weekends with?
>
> Rita Rudner

Is marriage an outdated concept?

Many people think it is because society has tried to make the square peg of marriage fit in the round hole of self-interest. People say marriage seems archaic, almost barbaric. Women protest, "I don't need a man! I have a good-paying job. I know how to change the oil in my car, or I can pay someone else to do it." And with the rise of the metrosexual, men are heard saying, "What do I need a wife for? I get more sex than married men. I know how to dress. I am a gourmet chef. I wrote the book on interior design. What would a wife add to the equation?" And with that, marriage has become more than outdated; it's almost obsolete. What used to be essential—having a partner to do the things you don't do—is now unessential. Or perhaps it's a luxury that many successful people just can't afford without a prenup.

But what *Marriable* is about is the idea that marriage still has a lot to offer when formed according to its original definition. Marriage was created as a partnership, two strands being stronger than one. Marriage was also created for family. Children growing up in single-parent households are at a significantly increased risk for drug abuse as teenagers.[9] While the earth has been successfully populated (and in some places overpopulated), having children is now viewed as a way to acquire desired possessions or hobbies instead of an obligation to create and raise the next generation of leaders, artists, doctors, and so on who will take care of and rule over the planet.

But since you read this book, we probably don't have to convince you of the benefits of marriage. You probably have a big list of things you hope to get out of it. You might even classify them as needs, things you have to get in order to feel fulfilled and loved. The list might include things like sexual fulfillment, companionship, romance, affection, financial security, physical safety, family, and entertainment. A recent study shows that compatibility across all of these areas is important in having a marriage that lasts—even more important than having moral values in common. Some dating websites even offer ways to help ensure complete compatibility in an attempt to divorce-proof your marriage.

Yet many a marriage has ended because one or more of these needs has not been met. People start getting divorced when they don't get what they want. What happens if you marry for romance and suddenly your partner loses his romantic streak? Did you marry the wrong person? Is a no-fault divorce coming your way? Many people claim that "we just grew apart," "my needs weren't being met," and the list goes on. But is meeting your needs really what marriage was meant for? Or is there perhaps a bigger picture, a bigger purpose for marriage that is being overlooked? These might be your needs for a happy marriage, but to base whether you stay married or not on the fulfillment of these needs is a false marriage contract. The focus of our commitment should be not on fulfilling our needs but on fulfilling the other's needs. And that helps keep the marriage from failing.

Some singles have responded to this marriage culture crisis by saying, "I'm just going to wait for the one God has chosen for me. My serendipitous soul mate." They argue that when you're a child, your mother says, "If you get lost, stay in one place and wait and I'll find you," and we're running around not waiting for God to bring us the one he's chosen for us. But all that these well-intentioned singles are doing in trying to protect themselves from getting too involved with the wrong one romantically is over-romanticizing what God is going to do. They're making a romantic event out of God choosing someone for them, and they're losing sight of what marriage was created for. Marriage is not this big romantic thing, like "God has chosen this one for me to make my life complete and give me all of my wants and needs and desires." Marriage is anything but hands free or automatic, so why should the dating process be anything less?

Giving Up Singleness Is Hard to Do

Studies show that between 70 and 90 million Americans are not presently married. A lot of those people think, or claim to think, that singleness is the greatest invention since sliced bread. But not you! Buying this book is proof of that, right? These eternally single-minded covet their freedom to make their own decisions. They see marriage as a losing proposition. You lose on picking where you're going to eat, you lose in the video store, you lose on arranging the furniture. Truth is, unless you married a doormat, you can't avoid losing. But that's only a surface understanding of marriage. Could it be that the single who covets the power to control their own life is missing out on the greatest adventure of a lifetime by avoiding the bonds of marriage? The truth is that most singles just can't avoid that secret mystery of life that gnaws at us deep inside, that sense that life just can't be all about me and what I want. A greater story must be out there—one that involves more than just me and my desires and needs.

You've Got Quotes X

"There's got to be more to life than chasin' 'round every temporary high to satisfy me."
Stacie Orrico

Cohabitable

Living together, or "shacking up," as some might call it, has become a modern epidemic. On the surface it seems to incorporate the best of both worlds, marriage and singleness. But dig a little deeper and you'll see that it simply removes the benefits of both worlds and opts for a deformed mix of sex and comingling of assets without security. And women have the most to lose due to the simple fact that they run the risk of pregnancy and the subsequent raising of children, while men run no permanent risk at all to their way of life. Some women think the great coup of the sexual revolution was that women can now decide for themselves whether

Cohabitation Is Nutty

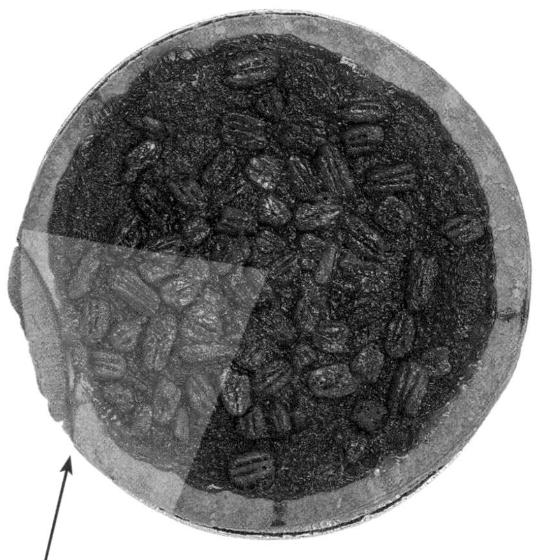

"About 20 percent of all male-female cohabitors, or 1.6 million people, have been living together for more than five years."[12]

"There are 9.7 million Americans living with an unmarried different-sex partner."[10]

"Cohabitation before first time marriages is associated with a greater chance of divorce."[11]

they will marry or simply shack up. And they mistakenly call this freedom. Perhaps a better word for it might be *manipulation*.

An honest look inward reveals that the average woman cohabitates with the hope that living with *her* will drive *him* to want to marry. She lies to herself that this step of living together will be the last step before marriage and will really help him to see that he can't live without her and must live with her in the bond of marriage. Unfortunately, the main thing the man wants from a relationship with a woman—sex—is now being given away as if it weren't the biggest bargaining chip she has.

Michael,

Been there, done that. Let me just add that it lightens up his romance load too. When you move in with a woman, you no longer have to work on the romance to keep her around. It really lets the guy off the hook romantically. And now the only tool left for the woman to get him to commit is guilt or "accidental" pregnancy.

Hayley,

But something seems so romantic to a woman when we hear him say, "So, you wanna move in together?" We can build romance on that for weeks.

When you pull the pin on the cohabitation grenade, for that short honeymoon period, you're playing the role of some black-and-white TV series from the '50s. You're writing out shopping lists, redecorating, throwing dinner parties . . . but before long the fuse burns out, and her charming quirks become irritating habits.

Now, let's take a look at the other half of the equation. Ask any guy what he would do if he had the choice between buying a car and being able to test drive it for two years without paying. He'll take the test drive option every time. Most guys shack up because they like the free sex, the better furniture, and only having to pay half the living expenses. And besides, she beats the roommate who considers cleanliness a foreign concept.

What the woman wants and most of the time gets out of marriage is the security of commitment. It's a security that assures her that if she were to get pregnant, she would have a partner, a mate, who would support her and be with her through the birth and raising of the child. If what the man wants out of marriage is a sexual partner, some home cooking, and a clean house, he can get all that out of shacking up, plus the add-on that he only has to pay half the rent and utilities, and all without any commitment. The man wins hands down in cohabitation. He can get out of cohabitation almost the same thing he would get out of marriage, while the woman gets almost nothing of what she desires. Cohabitation is a losing proposition for the woman. And for the man it's a gentleman's agreement for services that no gentleman would take. A boy cohabitates, but a man steps up and makes a commitment.

Michael,

When a guy says that, he's dissecting what marriage is and only giving you a piece of it. He's giving you a bite of the cheesecake instead of the whole slice.

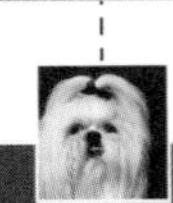

Hayley,

I've been there, done that too, and once I got the key to his place, I did really easily lie to myself and enjoyed playing house. I never really considered that it would end just like every other dating relationship.

Remarriable?

Whether you're divorced, your love interest is divorced, or one or both of you has lived with a "significant other," a broken marriage or broken simulated marriage is baggage that needs to be factored into any dating relationship. When a new customer walks into a bank for a loan, the first thing the loan officer will do is pull a credit report to look for patterns of fiscal responsibility (or irresponsibility). A late payment here and there might not raise an eyebrow. A period of habitual late payments followed by a recovery period might need some explanation, but a significant recovery period should be enough for the loan. A bankruptcy? The loan officer's arms suddenly fold across her chest. If the one you are dating has a divorce in their past, they have some explaining to do; they just need to go through a much more rigorous application process than the average person applying for a loan, er, date. In the age of no-fault divorces, finding a suitable mate who doesn't have one "under their belt" is harder and harder as you get older. So what to do? Is there a tried and true formula for knowing that they've learned their lesson and the next one is forever?

Marriage Enemy #1

Numerous marriage and family counselors believe that the number one predictor of divorce is the habitual avoidance of conflict. At first couples avoid conflict because they are so much in love and believe that "being in love" is about agreeing. Disagreeing with the other person can quickly defog your love goggles if you believe the myth that if couples disagree or fight, they'll ruin their relationship.

Later, conflict builds because dealing with differences gets so out of hand that fights become destructive. Conflict turns the avoider's world so inside out that they basically shut down. After a few big eruptions, they are even more determined to avoid conflict at any cost.

Successful relationships come from knowing how to discuss differences in ways that actually strengthen the relationship. This builds intimacy far more than any candlelight dinner or midnight stroll. Couples learn they can trust each other enough to disagree and still enjoy a life of commitment to each other.

Our advice here is that if the divorced party is blaming their ex or sees the decision they made to divorce as the most "freeing" decision of their life, beware.

The Purpose of Marriage

We're going to talk about the purpose of marriage in two distinct categories. This is because men and women are different, and anyone who tells you otherwise has been brainwashed. Marriage is successful because it bonds two unique elements. It's like this: combine the elements of hydrogen and oxygen in the right way, and you no longer have hydrogen and oxygen—you have water. Because

Confessions of a Lemon

by Michael

When what appears to be a perfectly good car repeatedly breaks down for no apparent reason, the auto industry calls that car a "lemon." We too can encounter or even become a "lemon" ourselves in our relationships.

I, Michael, have a confession to make. Over the course of one failed marriage in my early twenties, two decades of dating, and three live-in girlfriends, I became a signature lemon. Consistently showing promise early on, I could eloquently explain away the circumstances of my repair history to the latest love interest. But inevitably I would soon inexplicably break down, leaving the other person broken as well, stranded in the middle of nowhere with hitchhiking or calling the auto club her only prospect of getting back to relationship civilization.

Not until I seriously took a hard look at who my actions said I was, instead of just my twisted view of who I hoped I was, did I finally get it. Without pointing fingers at others, I fell to my knees and committed myself to a view of relationships and marriage the way God intended: one wife for life.

Hayley,

You know what? I knew you weren't a lemon anymore when you told me that the greatest mistake you had ever made had nothing to do with lying or stealing but was getting a divorce. To me, it spoke volumes that even though you would never get back together with your ex, you felt divorce was the gravest mistake of your life because marriage was a promise for life.

Michael,

I just knew that you couldn't possibly trust that the promise I might make to you for life would mean anything unless you knew I saw that decision to divorce as fundamentally wrong. I thought it was important for you to know that instead of just saying, "It just didn't work out."

of their elemental differences, men and women each get different things out of the marriage union, regardless of how they arrange their marriage. Sociologically, historically, and even spiritually, men and women derive distinct benefits from the

INSTANT MESSAGE
from haze@marriable.com

For excellent resources with a *Marriable* approach to dating after divorce, dating for the single parent, and related topics, log on to www.marriable.com.

marriage union, and whether or not times have changed, the core benefits can still be seen.

The Purpose of Marriage for Women

Protection—Historically, marriage has provided physical protection for women in the face of violence, wild animals, and starvation. But even now marriage provides a certain degree of financial, physical, and even emotional protection for women that can't be denied. (HD: Before I was married I was scared every night and flinched at every sound I heard. Now that I am married the fear is gone. I know that if someone breaks in, they have to contend with Michael. It's a great deal of safety for me.)

The porpoise de marriage.

Sexual intimacy—The woman also gains a degree of protection when it comes to intimacy. She is much more protected from heartache in the marriage union than in the casual dating relationship. This protection, provided by commitment, can allow her to explore all her sexual desires and enjoy her sex life to the fullest.

Children – Marriage also offers protection for her children. Women who give birth outside of marriage struggle more financially, emotionally, and physically (toting around a fat three-year-old) than women who have a partner to share the burden with them. Not only that, but children benefit from two-parent homes in ways that can barely be calculated.

Financial support – Even though in today's day and age many a woman makes more than her husband, on the whole men earn considerably more than women. When two incomes are brought together, both male and female benefit. Bill Harley, author of *His Needs, Her Needs,* claims that a woman's number four top need is for the financial security that a man provides. You can scream against this all you want, but the truth is that women derive a good deal of comfort from knowing they have a man who can support them if need be. And if a woman intends to have children, this need really grows.

Companionship – Another key ingredient to a happy life for a woman is companionship. Marriage provides a woman with certain companionship for her long nights and short weekends.

The Purpose of Marriage for Men

Sexual fulfillment – Do we really need to explain this one? Really?

Nine out of ten men said sex was the number one reason they got married.

But wait! This just in: the tenth man's ballot was disqualified due to the fact that his wife filled out the questionnaire for him. The investigation was initiated after his response *"having someone to share my dreams with"* was invalidated.

Peace – Most single men will admit that they feel a degree of restlessness in their lives. They never quite feel settled down until they find themselves a wife, and then marriage serves the purpose of taking away that restlessness. Men tend to be wanderers, not nesters, and bringing a woman into the equation can help him to feel more connected to his community and settled into his life.

Motivation – The *New York Times* recently reported that married men earn between 10 and 50 percent more than single men. Perhaps this is because the marriage partner gives him a degree of motivation that he didn't have in his singleness. Suddenly someone else is out there depending on him. This can often drive men to seek success much more than just an empty apartment ever could. We also can't discount that having a permanent fan base increases a man's confidence and therefore his success. Marriage is the perfect environment for the financial and overall success of the man, motivating him to be all he can be.

Maturity – Not to dis the single guys, but a degree of maturity comes with marriage. Perhaps it is the sense of responsibility and the depth that comes along with relating to a wife. Oftentimes one finds that women "tame" men to some degree. She makes sure he doesn't leave the house "looking like that." She helps

The "Danger" of Avoiding Premarital Sex

by Michael

When I told a counselor friend of mine that Hayley and I were waiting for marriage before "doing the deed," he strongly cautioned me about "the dangers of waiting" and the problems that would face us in marriage because we hadn't worked through our sexual relationship. While he had been an invaluable help for me in rebuilding my life after addiction, on this one topic I chose to listen to my moral compass.

HD: Of course, he was a man! Sure, get as much premarital sex as you can, 'cuz after marriage your chances of getting any go way down, right?

the way he communicates and behaves around others. She just makes him more presentable. (HD: When I was single and hanging out with a group of singles, I noticed that the kind of dorky guys—the ones who acted like little boys, dressed like teenagers, and seemed the least mature of them all—suddenly changed once they got married. Their dress became more mature. Their behavior grew up, and they looked less like boys and more like men. Marriage matures.)

Most anthropologists (and many online dating services) will tell you that compatibility and sharing the same perspective on the meaning of marriage are why arranged marriages are so successful—because the matches are arranged based on economic or objective compatibility concerns instead of stomach butterflies and goo-goo eyes. So do we throw out all hopes for romantic love and marry the person who "makes the most sense"? We say an unapologetic, "No way, Jose." Romance was a big catalyst in our dating relationship, and that's important. But we knew that when we hit hard times ahead, our common perspective on marriage would have to hold us together—and that's even more important.

Hayley,

Honestly, marriage is the best thing that's ever happened to us, right, Michael? Hey, wipe that blank look off your face!

Michael,

Just kidding. Yes, yes, it's the best thing that's ever happened in my life. Just the act of marriage wasn't what did it, because I had already tried it once and it didn't change my life for the better. But coming into marriage with a healthy definition of what marriage is and realizing that I had to be *Marriable* and start dating *Marriable* people made the difference between taking the *Titanic* and the *Love Boat*.

We truly believe that marriage is an experience like no other, where we are faced with our biggest flaws and where we fall short so that God can help us grow into the person we were created to be. Something is freeing about the thought that marriage was created as a curing process. Through the life of your marriage, you're sure to be cured of all illusions that the world revolves around you and what you want. That's real freedom and real love. Serving and caring for someone in spite of their faults because you made a lifelong commitment to them—there's your romance.

So, Grasshopper, marry for love. Marry for purpose. Marry for partnership. Marry for life. Now you can take the desperate out of dating. Now you know how to be *Marriable.*

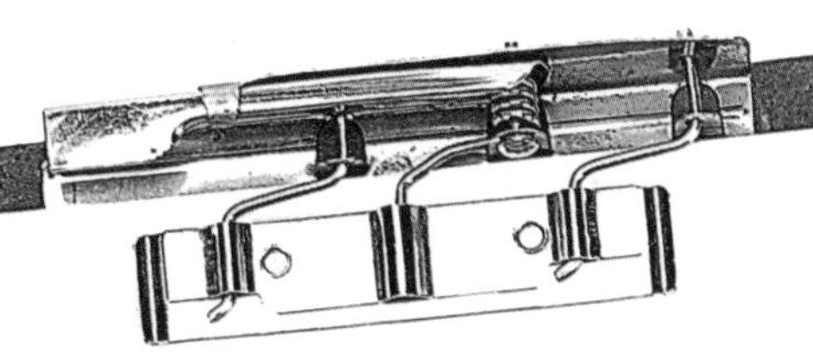

Suggested Reading List

Arterburn, Steve, et al. *Every Man's Battle*. Colorado Springs: Waterbrook, 2000.

Arthur, Kay. *A Marriage without Regrets*. Eugene, OR: Harvest House, 2000.

Harley, Willard F. Jr. *His Needs, Her Needs*. Grand Rapids: Revell, 2001.

Kline, Steven D., and Amy Frome. *Rate Yourself on Romance*. New York: Pedigree Books, 2002.

Leman, Kevin. *The Birth Order Book*. Grand Rapids: Revell, 2004.

Means, Patrick. *Men's Secret Wars*. Grand Rapids: Revell, 1999.

Warren, Neil Clark. *How to Know If Someone Is Worth Pursuing in Two Dates or Less*. Nashville: Nelson, 1999.

Notes

1. Helen Fisher, *Why We Love* (New York: Henry Holt, 2004), 183.

2. Family Safe Media, "Pornography Statistics 2003," http://www.familysafemedia.com/pornography_statis tics.html.

3. Victor B. Cline, Ph.D., "Pornography's Effects on Adults and Children," Morality in Media, 2001 http://www.moralityin media.org/index.htm?pornsEffectsArticles/clineart.htm.

4. Family Safe Media, "Pornography Statistics 2003."

5. Cline, "Pornography's Effects."

6. *Merriam-Webster's Collegiate Dictionary*, 10th ed., s.v. "Pornography."

7. Proverbs 4:23.

8. Vanderbilt University, "Women More Likely Than Men to Put Emotions in Motion," News and Public Affairs News Release, June 16, 1998, http://www.vanderbilt.edu/News/news/june98/nr4.html.

9. Rhonda E. Denton and Charlene M. Kampfe, "The Relationship between Family Variables and Adolescent Substance Abuse: A Literature Review," *Adolescence* 114 (1994): 475–95.

10. Larry Bumpass, James Sweet, and Andrew Cherlin, "The Role of Cohabitation in Declining Rates of Marriage," *Journal of Marriage and the Family* 53 (1991): 913–27.

11. Ibid.

12. Ibid.

Hayley DiMarco writes cutting-edge, best-selling books, including *Dateable: Are You? Are They?*, *The Dateable Rules*, *Mean Girls: Facing Your Beauty Turned Beast*, *Mean Girls All Grown Up*, *The Dirt on Dating*, and *The Dirt on Breaking Up*. From traveling the world with a French theater troupe to working for a little shoe company called Nike and then being the idea girl behind the success of the Biblezine *Revolve*, Hayley has seen a lot of life and decided to make a difference in her world. Hayley founded Hungry Planet, a publishing company that "feeds the world's appetite for truth." Hungry Planet helps organizations understand and reach the postmodern mind-set, while Hungry Planet books tackle life's everyday issues with a distinctly modern spiritual voice.

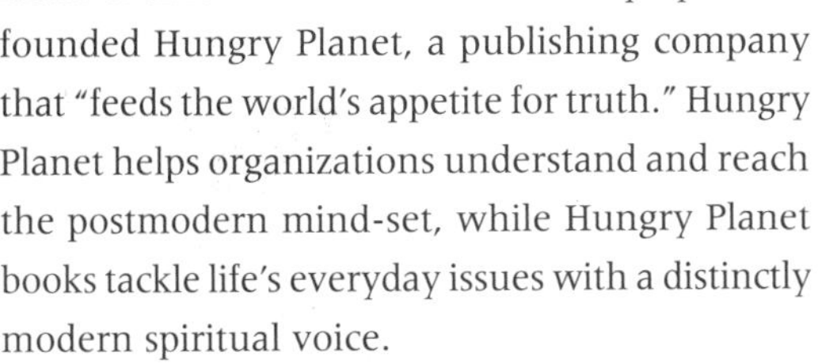

Michael DiMarco is general manager of Hungry Planet, a publishing company founded by his wife, Hayley, that works with fresh authors who want to reach an increasingly postmodern culture with premodern truth. Before helping manage Hungry Planet projects like *Mean Girls*, *The Gospel Unplugged*, and *Marriable*, Michael worked in publisher relations for an electronic publishing company, was a national speaker at pastors and Christian conferences, coached volleyball for seven years at the university level, wrote award-winning humor columns on relationships, worked in talk radio, and cohosted a relationship humor radio show called *Babble of the Sexes*. Michael and Hayley live in Nashville, Tennessee.

Hayley's back to help you cultivate friendships that leave MEAN *in the dust*

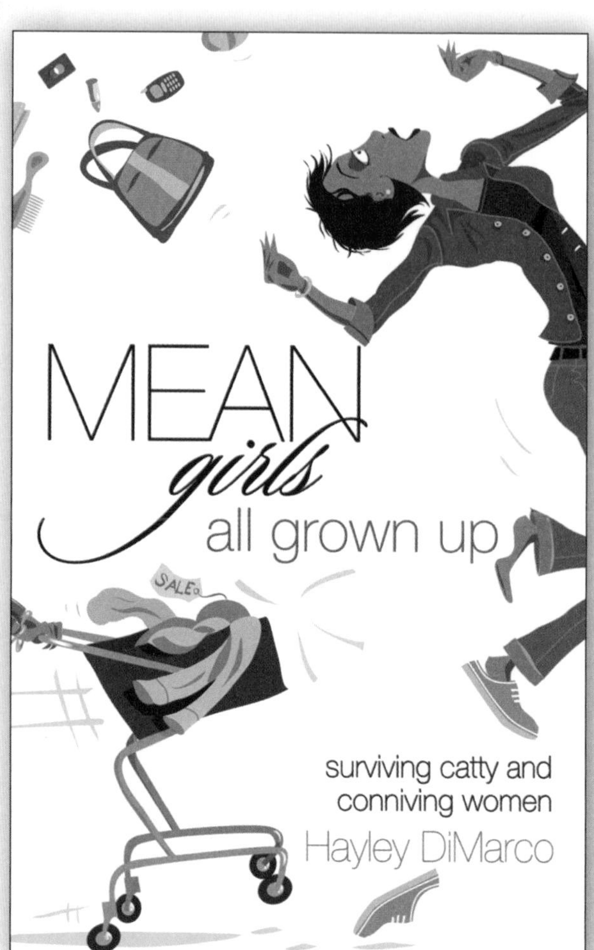

Catty Women Alert X

To rid yourself of this virus, please run MeanGirlsAGU.exe

What makes Hungry Planet books different?

Every Hungry Planet book attacks the senses of the reader with a post-modern mindset (both visually and mentally) in a way unlike most books in the marketplace. Attention to every detail from physical appearance (book size, titling, cover, and interior design) to message (content and author's voice) helps Hungry Planet books connect with the more "visual" reader in ways that ordinary books can't.

With writing and packaging content for the young adult and "hip adult" markets, Hungry Planet books combine cutting-edge design with felt-need topics, all the while injecting a much-needed spiritual voice.

Why are publishers so eager to work with Hungry Planet?

Because of the innovative success and profitable track record of HP projects from the best-selling *Dateable* and *Mean Girls* to the Gold Medallion-nominated *The Dirt on Sex* (part of HP's The Dirt series). Publishers also take notice of HP founder Hayley (Morgan) DiMarco's past success in creating big ideas like the "Biblezine" concept while she was brand manager for Thomas Nelson Publishers' teen book division.

How does Hungry Planet come up with such big ideas?

Hayley and HP general manager/husband Michael DiMarco tend to create their best ideas at mealtime, which in the DiMarco household is around five times a day. Once the big idea and scope of the topic is established, the couple decides either to write the content themselves or find an up-and-coming author with a passion for the topic. HP then partners with a publisher to create the book.

How do I find out more about Hungry Planet?

Use the web, silly—www.hungryplanet.net